LOUIS ARMSTRONG

The AFRICAN-AMERICAN BIOGRAPHY LIBRARY

GWENDOLYN BROOKS
"Poetry Is Life Distilled"
ISBN-13: 978-0-7660-2292-8
ISBN-10:   0-7660-2292-7

LANGSTON HUGHES
"Life Makes Poems"
ISBN-13: 978-0-7660-2468-7
ISBN-10:   0-7660-2468-7

MAYA ANGELOU
"Diversity Makes for a Rich Tapestry"
ISBN-13: 978-0-7660-2469-4
ISBN-10:   0-7660-2469-5

MUHAMMAD ALI
"I Am the Greatest"
ISBN-13: 978-0-7660-2460-1
ISBN-10:   0-7660-2460-1

RAY CHARLES
" I Was Born With Music Inside Me"
ISBN-13: 978-0-7660-2701-5
ISBN-10:   0-7660-2701-5

ZORA NEALE HURSTON
"I Have Been in Sorrow's Kitchen"
ISBN-13: 978-0-7660-2536-3
ISBN-10:   0-7660-2536-5

LOUIS ARMSTRONG

"Jazz Is Played From the Heart"

Michael A. Schuman

Series Consultant:
Dr. Russell L. Adams, Chairman
Department of
Afro-American Studies,
Howard University

Enslow Publishers, Inc.
40 Industrial Road
Box 398
Berkeley Heights, NJ 07922
USA
http://www.enslow.com

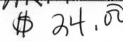

"JAZZ IS PLAYED FROM THE HEART. YOU CAN EVEN LIVE BY IT. ALWAYS LOVE IT."
—Louis Armstrong

Copyright © 2008 by Michael A. Schuman

Library of Congress Cataloging-in-Publication Data

Schuman, Michael.
    Louis Armstrong : "Jazz is played from the heart" / Michael A. Schuman. — 1st ed.
      p. cm. — (African-American biography library)
    Includes bibliographical references and index.
    ISBN-13: 978-0-7660-2700-8
    ISBN-10: 0-7660-2700-7
    1. Armstrong, Louis, 1901–1971—Juvenile literature. 2. Jazz musicians—United States—Biography—Juvenile literature. I. Title. II. Title: "Jazz is played from the heart".
    ML3930.A75S56 2007
    781.65092-dc22
    [B]   2006018654

Printed in the United States of America

10 9 8 7 6 5 4 3 2 1

To Our Readers:
We have done our best to make sure all Internet Addresses in this book were active and appropriate when we went to press. However, the author and the publisher have no control over and assume no liability for the material available on those Internet sites or on other Web sites they may link to. Any comments or suggestions can be sent by e-mail to comments@enslow.com or to the address on the back cover.

Every effort has been made to locate all copyright holders of material used in this book. If any errors or omissions have occurred, corrections will be made in future editions of this book.

Illustration Credits: American Memory, Library of Congress, pp. 18, 25; Associated Press, p. 108; Chicago Jazz Archive, p. 56; Everett Collection, Inc., pp. 80, 89, 100; Getty Images, pp. 37, 64 ; Hogan Jazz Archives, Howard-Tilton Memorial Library, Tulane University, New Orleans, Louisiana, pp. 7 (top center), 12 (top center), 14, 23 (top center), 35 (top center), 47 (top center), 62 (top center), 76 (top center), 93 (top center); iStockphoto.com, p. 50; Library of Congress, pp. 7 (top right and left), 12 (top right and left), 23 (top right and left), 35 (top right and left), 47 (top right and left), 62 (top right and left), 73, 76 (top right and left), 87, 91, 93 (top right and left); Louis Armstrong House & Archives at Queens College , pp. 27; Louisiana State Museum Jazz Collection, pp. 9, 11, 21, 29, 33, 71, 83; National Archives and Records Administration, pp. 5, 44; Photofest, p. 6; Satchmo.net, p. 59; Shutterstock , p. 42; Time & Life Pictures, Getty Images, p. 98; Twentieth Century Fox Film Corp./Photofest, p. 105.

Cover Illustrations: Everett Collection (lower right); Library of Congress (left).

Contents

Louis "Satchmo" Armstrong in the 1920s

◆◆◆◆◆

Chapter 1

The Telegram

The year was 1922, and Louis Armstrong was a young man with a gift.

He could play the cornet, an instrument similar to a trumpet, with a skill few others could match. His specialty was a new kind of music called jazz. Jazz had been developed gradually over the course of several years in his hometown of New Orleans, Louisiana.

Despite the popularity of jazz, it was not easy to earn a living playing that music. So Louis worked tiresome day jobs to earn needed money. At night he played the cornet in bands in clubs called honky-tonks. Most were located in crime-filled neighborhoods. To gain exposure for himself Armstrong also took advantage of a unique New Orleans tradition: funeral parades. The funeral parades gave him another opportunity to play in public.

Funeral Parades

Traditional jazz funerals in New Orleans begin with a service at a church or a funeral parlor. At its end, a marching jazz band meets the mourners. The band plays somber hymns while leading the mourners to the burial site for another religious ceremony. After the graveside service, the band leads the mourners away quietly. At what is considered a respectful distance from the gravesite, the band then plays up-tempo or even joyous songs. Relatives and friends take out fancy umbrellas and dance merrily behind the band. According to New Orleans jazz musician Ellis J. Marsalis, Jr., many of the umbrellas are "elaborately decorated," and "seem to be more about styling and profiling than protection from nature's elements." This group of dancers is called the "second line."[1] The tone celebrates the deceased person's life and the fact that he or she is now in Heaven.

One of Armstrong's best friends in the music business was an older cornet player named Joe (King) Oliver. In many ways, Oliver was more of a teacher to Armstrong than a friend. Like Armstrong, Oliver grew up in New Orleans, but by 1922 he was living in Chicago. Oliver had been a popular cornet player in New Orleans, but Chicago is a much bigger city. The big city gave Oliver more chances to grow in his career.

Louis Armstrong (left) poses with Joe (King) Oliver in 1923. While Armstrong and Oliver both played the cornet, Armstrong had recently started to play the trumpet.

Armstrong had had opportunities to move to bigger cities. However, he was a shy and guarded young man. Although he was twenty-one years old, he had never lived in any city other than New Orleans. He was very close to his grandmother, who had raised him, and his younger sister. To Armstrong, Chicago could have been on the dark side of the moon. He did not have the confidence to move from his hometown.

Because of that, Armstrong's career suffered. He was not making much money from playing music and the day jobs he worked were filled with drudgery. Still, the thought of moving away was terrifying.

Then on August 8, 1922, a hot, humid New Orleans day, Armstrong received a message that changed his life. He had just finished playing at a funeral and had gone home to change out of his sweaty band uniform. There he found a telegram from King Oliver. Oliver was inviting Armstrong to move to Chicago and play in his band.

Armstrong knew he would miss a huge opportunity if he turned down a chance to play with King Oliver. He had to make a decision: move to a strange city to further his career or stay near the comfort of his family.

Armstrong mustered all the courage he could and decided he was ready to take the big leap. The fact that the telegram came from his friend King Oliver was the clinching factor. Armstrong later wrote, "I had made up

King Oliver's jazz band performs on a sidewalk in San Francisco. From left: Ram Hall (drums), Honore Dutrey (trombone), King Oliver (cornet), Lil Harden, David Jones (saxophone), Johnny Dodds (clarinet), James A. Palao (fiddle), and Ed Garland (double bass). Soon, Louis Armstrong would join them.

my mind that I would not leave New Orleans unless the King sent for me."[2]

He would move to Chicago.

Louis Armstrong did not realize it then, but he would never have to work boring, menial jobs again. More importantly, after Armstrong's move north, the world of jazz would never be the same. Jazz historians say that Armstrong's life can be divided into two distinct periods: before he received Oliver's telegram, and after he received the telegram.

Chapter 2

Fish Head Stew, Red Beans, and Rice

Louis Daniel Armstrong was born in one of the poorest and toughest African-American neighborhoods of New Orleans. Gunshots echoed in the streets regularly and knife fights were common among its residents. Drugs and alcohol were a part of adults' lives. Because of the rampant crime that took place, the area was nicknamed the Battlefield. It was not a pleasant place to raise a child, but people who lived there had no choice.

For a long time, Armstrong's actual birthday was a mystery. As an adult, he claimed it was July 4, 1900. It seemed appropriate that a man who became a cultural ambassador for his country had a patriotic birthday. This was accepted by most of Armstrong's fans, but many jazz historians did not believe it was true. Whether or not

Armstrong believed it is unknown. For a long time, the majority of jazz historians guessed that Armstrong was born some time between 1898 and 1901.

Because few records were kept for poor African Americans, it was thought that no written record of Armstrong's birthday existed. Then in the early 1990s, the mystery was solved when a religious certificate recording Armstrong's baptism was discovered. It stated that Armstrong's actual birth date was August 4, 1901.

Although that question was finally answered, much is unknown about Armstrong's earliest years. His mother was named Mary Ann, but called Mayann. She was in her late teens when she gave birth to Louis. His father was named Willie Armstrong and he was in his mid-twenties when Louis was born. Within weeks after Louis's birth, Willie walked out on Mayann and Louis. He later married and had children with another woman.

Louis was left in the care of his grandmother, Josephine Armstrong, Willie's mother. Josephine lived in a small, one-story cabin. Louis had no toys and perhaps two or three pieces of clothing. Josephine could not afford to buy Louis shoes so he went barefoot much of the year. Blisters and bruises often covered his feet. Dinner consisted of meals only the poorest of the poor ate, such as fish head stew and red beans and rice.

> Blisters and bruises often covered his feet.

Josephine believed in discipline and was strict with Louis. When he misbehaved she would spank him with a switch from a chinaberry tree in her yard. Spanking was a was a common form of punishment at that time.

Two years after Willie Armstrong left Mayann, he returned to her. During that time they had a daughter named Beatrice who became known by the nickname Mama Lucy. Still, Louis continued to be raised by his grandmother.

Josephine was a religious woman. She belonged to a Catholic church but took Louis to services at both Catholic and Baptist churches. Thanks to his grandmother, Louis

This is the street that Louis Armstrong lived on with his grandmother. The buildings were eventually torn down.

became a singer in a church choir. It was his first experience performing for an audience.

As an uneducated African-American woman, Louis's grandmother did not have a lot of job opportunities. She earned a living doing laundry mostly for white people. Since she could not leave young Louis alone, Josephine took him with her to her jobs. He liked playing with the children of his grandmother's customers and loved the game of hide and seek. In those days, segregation was the law, and African Americans and whites generally did not mix often. But because of his grandmother's job, Armstrong became comfortable with white people at an early age.

> When Louis was five or six, he moved back with his mother to a tough neighborhood known as Storyville.

When Louis was five or six, he moved back with his mother to a tough neighborhood known as Storyville. He cried when leaving his grandmother, but Mayann needed him to watch over his baby sister Mama Lucy.

One day, Louis and his mother boarded a trolley on Tulane Avenue. Trolleys were a common method of intra-city transportation in the early 1900s. Louis grabbed a comfortable seat near the front of the trolley. Immediately, a trolley employee picked him out of his seat and dragged him to the back of the trolley car.

◆◆◆◆◆◆◆◆◆◆

Segregation

Segregation is separation of the races. This practice dated back to the Reconstruction years immediately after the Civil War. New Orleans was an exception to the rule in many cases. However, that changed after the United States Supreme Court decision *Plessy* v. *Ferguson* in 1896, in which the Court said "separate but equal" facilities for the races were constitutional.

African Americans were unable to ride railway cars or buses with white people. They could not use the same public bathrooms or drinking fountains. They were unable to stay in the same hotels or attend the same public schools. In many cases, they were not allowed to be treated in the same hospitals. Despite what the Supreme Court ruled, things might have been separate for the races, but they were not equal.

In the 1950s, United States Supreme Court decisions ruled against segregation. However, legal segregation did not truly end until laws banning it were passed in the 1960s. Even then, it took years before those laws were truly enforced.

She plunked him in a section under a sign that read, "For colored passengers only."[1]

As a small child, Louis did not know what he did wrong. He asked, "What do those signs say?" The worker responded, "Don't ask so many questions. Shut your mouth, you little fool."[2] It was Armstrong's first direct memorable experience with legal segregation.

Around the time Louis was six, he began attending the Fisk School for Boys. Like other schools in the South then, it was segregated. Armstrong learned to read and write there. He also began basic arithmetic. However, it is likely that he did not attend school often.

Armstrong was more interested in a different kind of education. He liked to visit a building across the street from his school. It was the Funky Butt Hall, a dilapidated honkytonk, or dance hall, where live music was played regularly.

Most of the bands in the honky-tonks played the blues. A new musical style called ragtime was also played at the Funky Butt. Ragtime is a syncopated, bouncy, piano-dominated music. It was originally known as "ragged time," because of its supposed ragged sound. Sometimes bands would play outside the honky-tonks to draw crowds before the actual dance started. Louis loved listening to the bands play outdoors. Once the dance started, he would walk to a side of the building and watch the bands through cracks in the walls.

In New Orleans when Louis was growing up, many musicians played in honky-tonks and juke joints (one is pictured above). They could often be rowdy and dangerous places.

New Orleans was and is a musical city. When Armstrong was small, bands played at all sorts of occasions. That included baseball games, the opening of businesses, and funeral parades. From the time Armstrong was a child, he was surrounded by music.

Being poor, Armstrong was constantly trying to earn money. Anything helped—a nickel here, a dime there. He sold newspapers with a white boy named Charles. Sometimes he collected potatoes and onions and sold them to restaurants. Other times, he resorted to petty theft and shooting craps, a dice game, on the streets.[3]

Louis also discovered he could earn money through singing. He formed a quartet with three other boys and sang on street corners. People who stopped to listen threw them coins. Each of the boys had a nickname. These included Big Nose Sidney, Little Mack, and Happy Bolton. Because Louis had a big, wide grin, the boys nicknamed him Hammockface, Dippermouth, and Gatemouth. The quartet performed together for at least a year, maybe two. Aside from earning money for Armstrong, these street performances gave him more experience singing for a live audience.

When Louis was about eight he went to work for the Karnofsky family. They were poor Jewish immigrants from Lithuania who lived in a ramshackle house not far from Louis'. The Karnofskys ran a business selling and delivering both coal and used goods that most people thought was junk. Included were items such as pieces of cloth, bottles, and scrap iron.

The Karnofskys had two sons who drove a horse-drawn wagon filled with their goods through the streets of New Orleans, looking for customers. The older son, Morris was twenty. The younger one was nineteen-year-old Alex. Morris and Alex took Louis on their wagon as they made their rounds through town.

> One day when he was riding in the junk wagon with the Karnofsky boys, he noticed a used cornet for sale in a store window.

To get the attention of potential customers, peddlers would shout or ring a bell as their horses clip-clopped through each neighborhood. Knowing Armstrong had some musical talent, the brothers had an idea. They gave Louis a crude tin and wooden horn to blow to draw people to their wagon. It was the kind of horn people use to celebrate holidays.

Armstrong experimented with the horn. He took off its wooden mouthpiece and placed two fingers close together where the mouthpiece had been. He discovered he could play lively and melodic tunes on that little horn. He entertained the Karnofskys' customers with his music as they came to the cart to trade bottles and rags for money.

Louis began to wonder what it would be like to play a real horn. One day when he was riding in the junk wagon

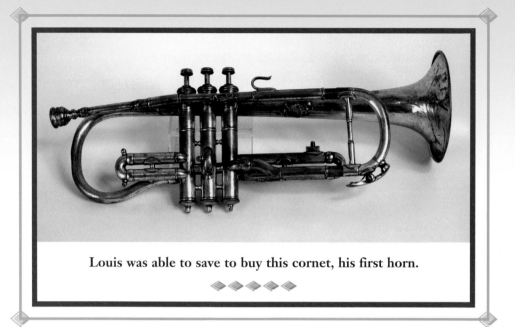

Louis was able to save to buy this cornet, his first horn.

with the Karnofsky boys, he noticed a used cornet for sale in a store window. He set his heart set on buying it.

The horn was priced at five dollars. Louis put aside 50 cents every week from the money the Karnofskys paid him for his work. The Karnofskys then gave Armstrong a two dollar advance on his salary. Thanks to the Karnofskys' help and Louis' budgeting, he was able to buy the cornet. "Boy, was I a happy kid." he said later.[4]

Morris Karnofsky helped Louis clean the grungy, old horn with brass polish. He also sterilized the inside with oil. Armstrong entertained the Karnofsky family by playing tune after tune such as "Home Sweet Home" and "Here Comes the Blues." The Karnofskys responded with rounds of applause.

Armstrong and the Karnofskys were becoming close. In some ways he was closer to them than to his mother, Mayann. They often hosted him for dinner and he acquired a taste for eastern European Jewish food such as matzo balls. He also learned by heart a Russian lullaby the Karnofskys' mother sang to her baby son, David. Soon, he was singing it along with her to the baby.

Through his interactions with the Karnofskys, Armstrong realized that Jews and African Americans had much in common as oppressed minorities in the United States. Armstrong wrote, "I had a long-time admiration for the Jewish people. Especially with their long time of courage and of taking so much abuse for so long."[5]

He was grateful throughout his life for the kindness the Karnofsky family showed him by helping him buy his first horn and by letting him join their family meals.

Chapter 3

Satchelmouth From Perdido Street

Between working for the Karnofsky family and singing for money in the streets, Louis found himself tired in the classroom during the day. When he was about eleven, Louis dropped out of school. His family needed money. His mother could not properly provide for him, and his father had almost nothing to do with him.[1]

Armstrong often earned money by performing on Poydras Street, a main thoroughfare in New Orleans, with friends Big Nose Sydney, Little Mack, and Happy Bolton. The group also came up with a new nickname for Louis: Satchelmouth. Like his old nicknames, the new one made good-natured fun of his sparkling, wide grin.

The quartet's act went beyond singing to include theatrics. Louis would sometimes dance a jig while his friends sang, and Happy amused people by doing somersaults. The quartet included skits in their act. In one, Louis fell to his knees, begging for a woman to love him. At the same time he would roll his eyes and make exaggerated facial gestures. After each act, the quartet passed a hat, and most of the time the audience responded by depositing money in it.

In time, Louis and his friends became familiar to established New Orleans musicians. One was Bunk Johnson, one of the city's best known and most talented trumpet players. Because Louis had a shy but cheerful nature, professional musicians in New Orleans took a liking to him. Johnson adopted young Louis as a protégé, allowing him to sit in with him when performing in public at regular gigs. The majority of those performances took place in the rough and tumble honky-tonks of Storyville.

> The honky-tonks were hardly the places where a boy of eleven should be hanging around.

The honky-tonks were hardly the places where a boy of eleven should be hanging around. But those were the places where Bunk Johnson and other musicians worked. When not playing his horn, Bunk took the time to teach Louis new songs and show him different ways to hold the cornet and use the mouthpiece. Despite the dangerous surroundings he was in, Armstrong managed to stay out of trouble.

That changed during a New Year's Eve celebration that has become legendary in Armstrong's life story.

Armstrong spent New Year's Eve 1912 singing with his quartet on the streets, which were filled with partiers welcoming in the new year with loud noises and bright lights. In 1912, that meant torchlight parades, fireworks, and even guns loaded with blank cartridges, even though the firing of guns was illegal.

Bunk Johnson played the trumpet his whole life. Here he is performing in Stuyvesant Casino in New York in June 1946.

Louis planned to celebrate with a .38 caliber pistol he found in his mother's cedar trunk.

Just after Louis fired his gun into the air, his friends ran off, leaving him alone. Louis turned around and saw a white police detective named Edward Holyland watching him. Holyland grabbed hold of Louis, who later remembered, "I started crying and making all kinds of excuses. 'Please, mister, don't arrest me . . . I won't do it no more . . . Please . . . Let me go back to mama. . . . I won't do it no more.'"[2]

A fifteen minute trial was held the next day, January 1, 1914. The judge, Andrew Wilson, heard Holyland's testimony and sentenced Louis to a school for troubled children called the Colored Waif's Home. It was run by a former soldier named Captain Joseph Jones. The term "colored," like the term "Negro," was used at the time for African Americans. A "waif" is a homeless child.

His sentence had no definite ending date. A judge would later decide when Armstrong would be released.

Although Louis' name would in the future appear in print thousands of times for his musical feats, it was first seen by newspaper readers in the daily *New Orleans Times–Picayune* under the headline, "FEW JUVENILES ARRESTED."[3]

The brief article read:

> Very few arrests of minors were made Tuesday, and the bookings in the Juvenile Court are no more than the average. Six white boys were arrested in Canal Street for disturbing the peace. The most serious case was that of Louis Armstrong, a twelve-year-old negro who discharged a revolver at Rampart and Perdido streets. Being an old offender he was sent to the negro Waif's home.[4]

During his first days at the waif's home, Louis was homesick and lonely for his mother and sister. He was so depressed that he refused to eat for three days.

This postcard shows the Colored Waif's Home. In the upper right, Captain Joseph Jones, the director at the time Armstrong attended, is pictured.

"On the fourth day," Armstrong later said, "I was so hungry I was first at the table. Mr. Jones and his colleagues gave me a big laugh. I replied with a sheepish grin. I did not share their sense of humor; it did not blend with mine."[5]

It did not take long for Louis to adjust to the group home. This was the first time that he had any kind of order in his life. He could now count on regular meals every day. For a boy used to scrounging for food, it was a treat. He also finally had clean clothing and comfortable shoes.

The Colored Waif's Home was run in a strict manner. Captain Jones used his military background as a model for the home. In addition to taking classes in which grammar and arithmetic were taught, the young residents took part in regular military drill. They were required to march on the grounds with wooden guns at least a few days a week.

The residents were expected to wash and iron their clothes, to make their own beds, and to scrub the floors. The boys also learned the skills of gardening. They grew vegetables and at dinner ate the produce they had grown.

As one might expect in New Orleans, there was music at the Colored Waif's Home. The home had its own band, led by a man named Peter Davis. Like the rest of the staff, Davis was African-American. Although he was a capable musician, it is believed he had no formal musical training.

Because Louis was from a rough neighborhood, Davis assumed the worst about him. He was tough on Louis at first. Armstrong later wrote:

> He would whip me every time he had a chance and every time he'd whip me he'd make these remarks. "You're one of those bad boys from Liberty and Perdido streets and I don't like you." So I figured there wasn't any use saying anything to him. I just stood there and took my beatings like a little man. Pretty soon I became afraid of him—every time he'd pass by me, at the dinner table or wherever it was, I'd get a cold chill. It was that way for a long time.[6]

Louis played in the Waif's Home band at the age of ten.
His face is circled in this picture.

In time, Davis began to warm up to the boy from Perdido Street. Davis realized that Louis was not a bad kid, but just from a tough neighborhood. He decided to give Louis a chance to prove himself and asked him to join the band.

The first instrument Davis gave him was a tambourine. New band members commonly began in the rhythm section. Davis next tried Louis on the bass drum, then the bugle. When Louis blew the horn, Davis knew he had a true talent on his hands. It was just a matter of time until Louis became the band leader.

Perhaps the best lessons band members learned had to do with discipline. When they performed well, Davis rewarded them with peppermint candies and ginger-bread cakes.

The boys did not play jazz, a style of music that was in its infancy and played in tough places like honky-tonks. Instead, they played brassy marches, patriotic songs, and old standards such as "Home Sweet Home" and "Swanee River." The first song Louis played in the Waif's Home band was a popular tune titled, "At the Animals' Ball."

The Waif's Home boys often played at private picnics or in city parades before both white and African-American audiences. They wore uniforms of long white pants, blue gabardine coats, caps with black and white bands, and black sneakers. And they loved taking their music all across town. Armstrong later wrote, "We were so glad to get a chance to walk in the street that we did not care how long we paraded or how far."[7] One day they marched twenty-five miles, playing their music the entire time.[8]

Throughout his life, Armstrong told different stories about his release from the Colored Waif's Home. He said at times that his mother Mayann, his father Willie, or both his parents together convinced a judge to release him.

Records show that Louis was released on June 16, 1914, which would have made him not quite thirteen.[9]

◆◆◆◆◆◆◆◆◆◆

The Beginnings of Jazz

Some genres of music, such as rock and roll and hip hop, evolved over the course of about a decade. That was not the case with jazz.

Jazz has its roots in the 1820s, when both slaves and free blacks gathered at a place in New Orleans called Congo Square. There they enjoyed playing and listening to the music of their African heritage. Such gatherings would not have been allowed in most of the South. But New Orleans, with its French and Spanish colonial backgrounds, was not like the rest of the South. Some of these musicians played in bands that led funeral processions through the city. In time, they played spirituals, ragtime, and blues. They even put European-based military music into their performances. This mixture of different musical genres gradually developed into the earliest form of jazz.

Several jazz historians credit a trumpet player named Charles "Buddy" Bolden as the father of jazz. They claim that some time around 1905, Bolden took this new unnamed music which had been played on strings and arranged it for brass instruments. People began to call it "jass." Over time it became known as jazz.

Judge Andrew Wilson realized that Louis was a model resident who had excelled in the school's band and was not a disciplinary problem.

Louis was placed in the custody of his father, Willie, and his stepmother, Gertrude. Louis had never met his stepmother and was concerned about how she would treat him. He grew to like her, but did not like his role in his father's house. Willie and Gertrude had two pre-teen sons named Willie and Henry. Louis soon learned he was expected to be a caretaker of his stepbrothers while Gertrude worked. He was not thrilled to spend his days taking care of and cooking for two younger boys.[10]

That job ended soon afterwards when Gertrude gave birth to a daughter. Willie sent Louis back to live with Mayann in the house on Perdido Street. Louis never went back to school. He spent his days drifting from one odd job to the next. He delivered milk for a dairy company for a while. He also took job as a stevedore, loading and unloading cargo ships. He even returned to selling newspapers.

The job he held the longest was delivering coal for a company located on Perdido Street, just a few blocks from his home. Louis was responsible for filling mule-driven wooden carts with about a ton of coal, then delivering it to customers. He was paid fifteen cents a day and often loaded and delivered five loads daily.[11] Some customers

Kid Ory

Kid Ory was one of the earliest jazz greats. He was born in a small town outside New Orleans probably between 1886 and 1890. Kid learned to play several instruments when he was a child, including guitar and trombone. He was a natural leader and started several bands as a teenager. Of all the instruments he could handle, Ory settled on playing the trombone professionally.

Like Louis Armstrong, young Ory made a point of heading to Storyville to hear live jazz. He ended up moving to New Orleans and formed a new band. Around 1912, Ory

began to hire himself out to play jazz at picnics, dance clubs, and private parties, especially those given by well-to-do white people. By 1915, there were few jazz fans in New Orleans who did not know the name Kid Ory.

Ory had a successful career for many years. Late in life he retired in Hawaii, where he died in 1973.

tipped him a little extra money or at times rewarded him with a free bite to eat.

Though Louis earned steady money from his various day jobs, at night he continued to hang around New Orleans' honky-tonks. His favorite place was Pete Lala's Cabaret, home to Edward "Kid" Ory's band. Ory's lead cornet player was none other than King Oliver.

Louis was intrigued by the heavyset and talented King Oliver. Armstrong later wrote, "Everybody was playing cornet then, but 'King' Oliver, 'Papa Joe' to me, was way out in front of all of them as the very best."[12] Oliver grew to know Louis well. Louis, with his charm and shyness, did not seem to be a threat to Oliver, which allowed the usually untrusting Oliver to take him on as an unofficial apprentice.

Armstrong was about to receive an education in music that exceeded anything he could have received in school.

Chapter 4

Fate Steps In

Whenever King Oliver needed an errand run or someone to carry his cornet case as he marched in a New Orleans street parade, he knew just the person to call: Louis "Satchelmouth" Armstrong. Louis was enthusiastic about helping the big man. He would also go out of his way to run errands for Oliver's wife, Stella. In response, she and King often had Louis over for dinner.

Louis had more than meals on his mind. In exchange for doing odd jobs, Louis asked Oliver for advice on playing the cornet. Oliver was happy to reward Louis with lessons, and it was just a matter of time until Oliver asked Ory if Louis could take his place on stage during breaks. Not long after that, Oliver allowed Louis to cover for him on nights he had double booked himself, or agreed to play in two different nightclubs on the same night.

Though Louis was learning from Oliver, he was also developing his own style. Oliver had grown up with ragtime music, and his style was basic and more constrained, as was fitting with ragtime. Louis came of age when ragtime was dying out, and he was more experimental with his cornet than Oliver.

Oliver may have been Louis' main mentor, but he was not his only one. His work delivering coal in Storyville allowed Louis to meet other musicians there. One was "Black Benny" Williams, a tough drummer who stood about six foot, six inches tall and was a mass of muscle. Louis befriended Williams since young Louis needed a protector on Storyville's mean streets. When Louis was invited to march and play in a second line following a funeral or street parade, Black Benny was often there beside him. Benny tied himself to Louis with a stretch of rope, and the two marched side by side—Louis playing the cornet, Williams on the bass drum.

Louis continued to work his day job. Playing music for money was unreliable, and the wages for musicians were not much better than they were for coal delivery men. At least when delivering coal Louis had steady income.

Two big events beyond Louis' control were about to affect his life. One was World War I, which the United States entered in April 1917. Louis was only fifteen years old at the time, too young to fight in the war. But the war had an indirect effect on his life.

During the war, many Navy men were stationed in New Orleans. After several of them were mugged, robbed,

Louis Armstrong poses for a portrait with his mother, Mayann (center), and his sister, Beatrice, in 1918.

and even murdered in Storyville, Secretary of the Navy Josephus Daniels demanded that the entire Storyville district be closed. On November 12, 1917, prostitution in Storyville was banned, and the police went door to door informing the residents.

One other occurrence that changed the lives of African-American jazz musicians was known as the Great Northern Migration. Tired of dealing with legal segregation and a lack of job opportunities in the South, tens of thousands of African Americans moved to northern cities to take jobs that would otherwise have been filled by immigrants. While they settled in many localities, the majority went to Chicago.

Around this time, Americans were purchasing phonographs, or record players, in large numbers. That meant that people all over the country could hear the new jazz music that came out of New Orleans. After hearing the music on a record, they wanted to hear it live. Jazz musicians in the South knew they could get jobs playing music elsewhere. One of the first to leave New Orleans was King Oliver, who headed north to Chicago.

Louis then became first cornet in Ory's band. However, after Ory moved to Los Angeles in 1919, Louis had to struggle on his own to find gigs to play at night. Of course, he still kept his day job delivering coal. He also discovered that trumpeters were more in demand than cornet players, so he switched to playing trumpet.

The Brick House in nearby Gretna was one of his frequent gigs. Louis Armstrong later said it was, "one of the toughest joints I ever played in."[1] Its customers were mostly men who did hard, drudge work on the levees. Armstrong said, "Those guys would drink and fight one another like circle saws. Bottles would come flying over the bandstand like crazy, and there was lots of plain common shooting and cutting. But somehow all of that jive didn't faze me at all, I was so happy to have a place to blow my horn."[2]

One other reason why Louis Armstrong may have enjoyed returning to the Brick House was twenty-one-year-old Daisy Parker, who worked there. Louis was falling in love with her. Parker had a boyfriend Louis did not know about. One day he caught Parker and Louis together and a fight broke out.

Rather than get in the middle of a woman and her jealous boyfriend, Louis decided to have nothing more to do with Parker. Although he was heartbroken, he felt it was for the best. A month after they broke up, Parker went looking for Louis at his home on Perdido Street. She told Louis she was in love with him, and the couple had a long talk. The next day they went to City Hall and got married. They set up a home in a two-room apartment in a poor New Orleans neighborhood.

From the start, their marriage was not a happy one. Daisy was a jealous and short-tempered woman, and the couple often came to physical blows. The only real pleasure

Louis seemed to get during his life with Daisy was from his cousin Flora's son, Clarence. Flora was poor and unmarried when she gave birth to Clarence, so Louis began to take care of the small child. He more or less adopted Clarence, treating him like a son.

One rainy day Clarence was playing on the back porch of Louis and Daisy's apartment building. He slipped on the slick porch and fell one story to the ground, landing on his head. Clarence was rushed to a hospital. He survived, but would be developmentally disabled for the rest of his life.

Louis was unable to support his family of Daisy, Clarence, Mayann, and Mama Lucy by playing trumpet and delivering coal. He felt he would be able to make more money selling the coal directly, rather than delivering it for someone else. At the same time, he still continued to get a few gigs a week.

> Early in 1919, Louis was playing trumpet on the back of a truck advertising a concert.

Early in 1919, Louis was playing trumpet on the back of a truck advertising a concert. He was watched by a tall, thin, man of mixed African and Irish descent named Fate Marable. Marable was a keyboard player who conducted a twelve-piece orchestra on riverboats that sailed the Mississippi River. They specialized in popular dance music rather than hot jazz.

Marable was a serious musician who, unlike Armstrong and many of the New Orleans musicians, could read music. He had first heard Satchelmouth Armstrong play with Kid Ory's band. Marable had been impressed by Louis's raw talent. Now Marable had a special offer to make to Louis. He wanted Louis to join his band on the riverboats.

In the winter of 1919 Armstrong played on riverboat excursions that sailed in and around New Orleans. But once the weather warmed up, the riverboat owners—four brothers named Roy, Joseph, John, and Verne Streckfus—sailed their ships further north up the Mississippi to entertain people who lived in Missouri, Iowa, and Minnesota. Marable wanted Louis to stay with his band and travel on these overnight excursions.

Staying overnight on the riverboat was not as scary to Louis as moving to a new, faraway city. He would be with musicians he had gotten to know, and he would always return home to New Orleans.

By this time, Louis and Daisy's marriage was crumbling. Louis had moved back into his mother's house. Still, Louis asked Daisy for permission to travel with Marable's band. A jealous woman, she was hesitant to let him go. Louis persuaded her by saying he could not continue to turn down good opportunities to advance his music career. So finally, she gave him permission to leave her and play on the riverboats.[3]

◆◆◆◆◆◆◆◆◆◆◆

The Riverboat Era

From the early to late 1800s the rivers of inland America were the nation's highways. Homes built alongside rivers often faced the water rather than a carriage road since the riverboat was the main source of moving both freight and people. The first steamboat on the Mississippi

is thought to have been the *Zebulon M. Pike*, which sailed out of St. Louis in 1817. Within twenty years, anyone could see more than one hundred riverboats docked alongside piers on the Mississippi, Missouri, Ohio, and other rivers. St. Louis residents recalled in 1850 they could see forests of smokestacks lined up on the Mississippi.

In the 1870s and 1880s, railroads were replacing riverboats as a quicker and more efficient means of carrying both passengers and goods. Yet Americans still longed for the colorful riverboats. In Armstrong's day they were used mainly for entertainment rather than practical purposes. Today, vacationers still cruise America's rivers on old-style riverboats for pleasure.

In the middle of 1919, Louis left New Orleans for the first time. His destination was St. Louis, where Marable's band had a temporary gig playing at a hotel. Mayann packed him a lunch: a fish sandwich and a bottle of green olives. When Louis Armstrong arrived in St. Louis, he acted like a lost child. A St. Louis-based pianist named Marge Creath recalled that Armstrong was so shy that he stood by himself, not speaking to anyone. Creath said, "I can see him right now; we were telling him how we loved his playing and he kept his head down, didn't want to talk."[4]

In time, Armstrong opened up to his fellow musicians and their fans. People would see the boat sailing up the river like a grand, floating wedding cake. Marable played the calliope, a keyboard-like instrument, signaling the boat's arrival. There was always an audience on the river-banks anxious to hear the lively music. The audiences on board the ships were respectful and well-behaved, and Armstrong liked that. It was a welcome change from the rowdiness of the New Orleans honky-tonks.

He also welcomed the discipline of Fate Marable. It was because of Marable that Armstrong learned to read music. Armstrong wrote:

> That's when—during our Intermissions—He [Fate] would help me out with my reading music. And me Being a very Apt young man, I learned a whole lots reading music Real Quick.—Fate Marable was a good Band Leader—And very Strict on us, when it came to playing that music Right.[5]

Armstrong played with Marable on the Streckfus brothers' riverboats for three years. By the fall of 1921, Armstrong had tired of playing a part in a large band. He had learned discipline by playing with Marable, but was now interested in blazing his own path. Marable allowed Armstrong to be the only band member to perform solos, but Armstrong wanted to take things one step further. He wanted to play music his way, and come up with his own style.[6]

The Fate Marable Band played on the S.S. *Capitol*.
Third from the right is Louis Armstrong, with his trumpet.
At the piano is Fate Marable.

At the same time, the boat's captain, Joe Streckfus, warned Fate Marable that his drummer Warren "Baby" Dodds, was breaking away from the band's standard rhythms. Dodds was improvising with bouncy and irregular beats. When Armstrong started adding his own creative twists to the riverboat band's standard repertoire, Streckfus ordered Marable to keep his brassy trumpet player under control as well.

> Chicago was much different than slow-paced New Orleans.

Dodds wanted nothing to do with those orders. He said about himself and Armstrong, "We were the stars on the boat. Why monkey with us?"[7] Dodds quit Marable's band. Inspired by Dodds' bold stance, Armstrong also resigned. Before long, Armstrong was back in New Orleans playing in honky-tonks and funeral bands.

It was in the summer of 1922 that Armstrong received Joe Oliver's telegram inviting him to play with his band in Chicago.

Chicago was much different than slow-paced New Orleans. It was a boisterous city whose residents were always in a hurry. New Orleans had a small town atmosphere compared to Chicago. Musicians who played in New Orleans seemed to have one goal: to entertain. Those who played in Chicago had a different goal: to make a lot of money. It would be easy for a shy and reserved man such as Armstrong to be taken advantage of in the big city.

King Oliver's band played under different names at different times but was best known as King Oliver's Creole Jazz Band. They performed in dance halls and cabarets, or small nightclubs. Most of the time they entertained crowds at a massive dance hall called Lincoln Gardens. As soon as Armstrong got off the train he took a cab to Lincoln Gardens where Oliver and the band were in the middle of a performance. The men recognized Satchelmouth right away.

Armstrong described his first impression of Lincoln Gardens. He said:

> It was a big place, with a big balcony all around, and I felt a little frightened, and wondered how I was going to make out. I knew it was such a big chance for me. I went on up to the bandstand and there were some of the boys I had known back home. They were glad to see me and I was tickled to death to see them all.[8]

How would Armstrong be able to make his way in a place so strange and so far from home?

Chapter 5

Up North

T hat night after Armstrong's first Chicago performance, Oliver took him home for dinner. Oliver's wife Stella prepared for Armstrong a meal of red beans and rice, bread, and lemonade. It was just like being back home in New Orleans.

After dinner, King Oliver took Louis Armstrong to a boardinghouse where Armstrong would live. When Oliver told Armstrong that he would have a private bath, Armstrong thought he was joking. He had never lived in a home that had a bathtub, to say nothing of a private bath. While Armstrong's new home was in a poor area on Chicago's south side, it was a step up from the poverty of New Orleans.

Armstrong spent several days with Oliver, rehearsing and familiarizing himself with the songs that the Creole Jazz Band played. Since he was second trumpet, he was

> Armstrong fit in well with the band, but after each show was over he returned to his empty room in the boardinghouse.

careful not to overshadow Oliver during performances. Yet Oliver did give Armstrong opportunities to shine with some powerful solos.

Armstrong fit in well with the band, but after each show was over he returned to his empty room in the boardinghouse. One night, Oliver asked Armstrong if he would like to meet a pretty jazz pianist who played in a different band in a Chicago club called the Dreamland Café.

Her name was Lillian Hardin and Armstrong was already familiar with her. Oliver had sent Armstrong a photograph of her when Louis was still in New Orleans. Based on the picture, Armstrong referred to Lillian as "an attractive looking, brown-skinned girl."[1] He told Oliver that he would like to be introduced to her but later confessed that he was "a little bit embarrassed" about actually meeting her in person.[2]

Lillian Hardin had a much different background than Armstrong. She grew up in a stable family in Memphis. She was a formally trained musician and had attended at least a year of college. She knew how to play the classical music of Bach, Chopin, and Mozart on the organ.

Like many young people in the early 1920s, she was intrigued by this new hot music called jazz. Her mother preferred Lillian play only classical music and hymns. Then the Hardin family moved to Chicago in 1918 as part of the great northern migration. Whether her mother liked it or not, Lillian was now exposed to jazz, which was heard all over the south side. Before long, Hardin was playing jazz professionally.

Although Louis and Daisy were still officially married, they were separated and had little to do with each other. After all, they were living 900 miles apart.

When Hardin met Armstrong, she thought he was unsophisticated, a fish out of water in the big city. She said:

> Everything he had on was too small for him. His atrocious tie was dangling over his protruding stom-ach and to top it off, he had a hairdo that called for bangs, and I do mean bangs. Bangs that jutted over his forehead like a frayed canopy. All the musicians called him Little Louis, and he weighed 226 pounds.[3]

Armstrong stood five foot, eight inches tall and for much of his life wrestled with his weight. At first, Hardin was not interested in the pudgy trumpet player who did not seem to know how to dress properly. In time, though, he won her over with his smile and personality. Soon Louis and Lillian were dating.

Lillian seemed to be just what Armstrong needed. Armstrong wrote, "Lil believed in me from the first. Being new in a big town and not being sure I could make good,

The Early Phonograph Industry

Thomas Edison invented the phonograph in 1877, but for decades it was considered just a toy—mainly a rich person's toy. In the 1920s, however, the United States was enjoying a burst of prosperity, and average consumers could now afford electronic products. That included phonographs, or record players. With middle income families now able to afford this luxury, the sales of records soared.

Edison's earliest phonographs hardly resembled the flat vinyl record common in most of the twentieth century. They were in the shape of cylinders and the stylus played sound by moving in an up and down motion. However, by the 1890s, inventors were experimenting with flat, disc-shaped records.

Phonograph records in both the disc and cylinder formats were made in the 1920s. Since discs were cheaper to make, the cylinder record industry gradually faded. The Edison Company made its last cylinder record in 1929. Vinyl disc records were the common form of recorded music until compact discs began to catch on in the 1980s.

her believing in me meant a great deal and helped me a lot."[4] She also took him clothes shopping and worked with him to lose weight. They were a happy couple.

Louis divorced Daisy, probably in 1922, and he and Lil were together all the time. In 1923 King Oliver's band was given a chance to take advantage of a wonder of modern technology: recorded music.

On April 5, 1923, Oliver's band traveled 250 miles to the town of Richmond, Indiana, home of the small Gennett Record Company. On that spring day in a one-story, wooden shack that had been converted into a recording studio, King Oliver's band recorded nine songs, including "Canal Street Blues," "Weather Bird Rag," "Froggie Moore Rag," and "I'm Going to Wear You Off My Mind."

Lillian said Armstrong played the trumpet so powerfully that he was forced to stand far from the rest of the band so he would not overwhelm them. She said, "He was looking so sad and I'd look back at him, smile, you know . . . Louis was at least 12–15 feet from us the whole session."[5]

One noteworthy result of the session was Armstrong's first recorded solo. It was in a song called "Chimes Blues."[6]

Another important result of the session was Lil Hardin's reaction to Armstrong's ability. She had thought for some time that he was too good to play second trumpet. When she saw him playing so strongly apart from the band she realized she was right. Lil said, "So then I was convinced. H'm yes, he really can play better because if his tone overshadows Joe [Oliver] that much he's got to be better."[7]

Armstrong and Hardin married on February 5, 1924. Soon afterwards, Lil urged Louis to break away from Oliver. She said he would not only make more money but could develop his talents to the fullest. Armstrong felt uneasy about leaving his mentor behind. He lacked the confidence to move forward.[8] But when some of Oliver's musicians began leaving to find other work, Armstrong finally took his wife's advice.

Armstrong took a new job playing first trumpet in a band led by drummer Ollie Powers. Less than a year later, he was contacted by a New York City-based bandleader named Fletcher Henderson. While Chicago was on the cutting edge of jazz, New York was the entertainment capital of the United States. Armstrong was well known among Chicago musicians, but he was hardly famous. Playing in New York could be good for Armstrong's career.

Few bands in New York played the pure jazz that had emerged out of the streets of New Orleans or in the clubs of Chicago. The New York bands played popular dance music. Now and then they would throw some jazz stylings into their songs, but that was as close to real jazz as they got. Most of these New York musicians were from families like Lil Hardin's. They were formally trained musicians who first saw jazz as a fad enjoyed by unrefined people.

Lil did not want to leave her work in Chicago, so Louis traveled alone to New York. He arrived in the city some time in September 1924. On October 7, 1924, Armstrong made his first record with Henderson's band. They played live gigs mainly in a hall called the Roseland Ballroom in the Broadway district of New York City. Now and then they entertained at private functions such as college fraternity parties. They also did shows at clubs in nearby states.

> Lil did not want to leave her work in Chicago, so Louis traveled alone to New York.

Armstrong played with Henderson's band just a little over a year. However, during that time Armstrong went through two major experiences that helped him grow as a performer.

The first had to do with his chance to work with blues legends. Playing with Henderson allowed Armstrong to play backup for distinguished blues singers such as Ma Rainey and Bessie Smith. Rainey and Smith have become legendary as two of the best-ever pioneering blues singers. It was common for blues singers to record with pickup bands and Fletcher Henderson had one of the best in New York. Many of these records are considered classics by jazz and blues historians today.

The second notable experience had to do more with Armstrong's voice than his trumpet. It was during

◆◆◆◆◆◆◆◆◆◆◆

Blues

The blues is a form of music with roots in African-American culture. The name comes from the term "blue devils," slang for a feeling of melancholy and depression.

Blues gradually evolved from African-American spirituals and the calls of field hands. The earliest forms developed in the 1890s. The blues grew out of what is known as call-and-response patterns in African-American music. In call-and-response, the musician sings a phrase which is answered by other musicians. The response might be vocal or instrumental.

Musically, basic blues is based upon a twelve-bar structure. Jazz, on the other hand, focuses on a melody created around a chord or perhaps a single note. Lyrically, blues tends to consist of stories about lost love, living under oppression, or tough times financially. However, some upbeat blues songs are about just the opposite, such as the wonderful emotion one feels when in love.

To use a gardening analogy, one might say blues is the stem, jazz is the fruit.

Armstrong's time with Henderson that he first sang a professional solo before an audience. The crowds as well as Armstrong's band mates loved hearing him belt out a song called, "Everybody Loves My Baby, But My Baby Don't Love Nobody But Me" in his trademark raspy voice.

Armstrong grew musically during his time with Henderson. But Henderson learned a lot about pure jazz from Armstrong as well. Before long Henderson's band had transformed themselves from a dance band to a swinging jazz band.

Lil and Louis kept in touch by mail. Lil encouraged Louis to convince Henderson to let him sing more often. In time Armstrong felt Lil was right and he became disenchanted with Henderson. Armstrong said, "Fletcher was so carried away with that society (stuff) and his education he slipped by a small-timer and a young musician—me—who wanted to do everything for him musically. I personally don't think Fletcher cared too much for me anyway."[9]

Armstrong left New York early in November 1925 and moved back to Chicago. He, Lil, and Clarence moved into a spacious, eleven-room house. Lil used her contacts in the nightclub business to arrange for her husband to play in the Dreamland Cafe. She also advertised Louis as "the world's greatest trumpet player."[10] Armstrong doubted himself and wondered if he could live up to that claim.[11]

An unidentified band plays at the Dreamland Café, where Lil Hardin set up some gigs for her husband Louis Armstrong.

While jazz was increasing in popularity, it was not accepted by everyone. Like most new styles of music, young people liked it before the general public latched on to it. In the 1920s, many felt jazz was crude music that belonged in the slums of New Orleans and Chicago. One concern was drug use. Drugs were used by many jazz musicians, and Armstrong smoked marijuana much of his life. On the other hand, a lot of whites considered jazz race music, or African-American music. Some of the more prejudiced whites believed that black society had a bad influence on white people. In fact, some genteel African Americans looked down on jazz, too.

The feeling of many towards jazz was summed up in a cartoon published in 1926 in a magazine called *Musical America*. In the cartoon, a boy wears a shirt with the word "JAZZ" written on it. A man is dragging the boy, kicking and screaming, into a concert hall featuring classical music. He says to the youngster, "Come on Buddy. I'll leave you with some real nice people."[12]

Regardless of what some thought of jazz, the music was not going away. Not long after Armstrong arrived in Chicago, he got word that the Chicago-based Okeh Record Company wanted to record some New Orleans jazz musicians. Okeh was founded by a German-American named Otto K. E. Heinemann in 1918 who named the label after his initials. By 1925, Okeh was a highly regarded recording company.

Armstrong put together a small band of his musician friends to cut some records in the Okeh studio. The group was called Louis Armstrong and His Hot Five, and they recorded many records over the next four years. Depending on how many musicians showed up for the recording sessions, they were sometimes tagged Louis Armstrong and His Hot Four or Louis Armstrong and His Hot Seven.

These combos never performed live; they only made records. But these records are regarded as classics today.

Some titles included the word "blues," such as "Potato Head Blues," "Keyhole Blues," and "Wild Man Blues." Others were "St. James Infirmary," a mournful, soulful ballad; "Strutting With Some Barbecue," inspired by a Chicago restaurant cook who fixed barbecue meals for Armstrong and other musicians; and "Cornet Chop Suey," which Armstrong named for another of his favorite types of foods, Chinese.

However, the record many jazz fans consider the best from Armstrong's Okeh recording sessions is "West End Blues." Some consider it the greatest trumpet recording ever.[13] Armstrong and His Hot Five recorded "West End Blues" on June 29, 1928. It begins with a powerful Armstrong trumpet solo. It then slows down as Armstrong sings in his gravelly voice, alternating with extended clarinet solos performed by Jimmy Strong and a piano solo by Earl "Fatha" Hines. Armstrong then comes in with another trumpet solo before the song reaches its conclusion. The last sounds heard are the clashing of the cymbals.

Fellow trumpet player Adolphus "Doc" Cheatham said, "You couldn't buy his [Armstrong's] records when they first came out. They were selling like hotcakes. Even grocery stores were selling his records."[14]

Around this time Armstrong had perfected a style known as scat singing. It is the practice of singing nonsense sounds rather than actual words. Scat singing might consist of sounds like, "Dee-bo, duh-deedle-la-bahm," and

Other members of the Hot Five, including Lil Hardin, gather around the piano at which Louis Armstrong is sitting.

"Rip-bip-ee-doo-dee-doot." Armstrong is believed to have first scatted in a song titled, "Heebie Jeebies."

A popular jazz legend is that Armstrong was recording "Heebie Jeebies" and the sheet music with the song's lyrics fell off the music stand. Instead of stopping the recording, Armstrong sang nonsense words as the band played on. Armstrong himself told that amusing story.

How did scatting really begin? There are many theories. Armstrong once told an interviewer that he and his friends sang scat on the streets of New Orleans when he was a child. Some historians believe that scat singing was developed by others long before Armstrong began singing. But even if Armstrong did not invent scatting, he certainly popularized it. Other jazz legends such as Cab Calloway and Ella Fitzgerald also became known for scat singing.

> As their relationship was crumbling, so was their working partnership. Armstrong started playing with other musicians.

When not recording, Armstrong continued doing live gigs. Yet performing with his wife was straining his marriage. In the 1920s, it was rare for a man to work for a woman, especially his wife. At home, Louis and Lil argued over petty issues. It is accepted by historians that neither was faithful to their marriage. As their relationship was crumbling, so was their working partnership. Armstrong started playing with other musicians.

At a Chicago theater called the Vendome, Armstrong became friendly with a nineteen-year-old female fan named Alpha Smith. Soon they were spending time together.

He also met someone else who would become important in his life. Joe Glaser was a concert promoter and night club manager. In 1927, he hired Armstrong and his combo to work at a Chicago club called the Sunset Café. Glaser was known as a tough promoter with close contacts to gangsters such as Al Capone. Many Chicago nightclubs were owned by gangsters.

Glaser immediately picked up where Lil left off, promoting Armstrong as, "The World's Greatest Trumpet Player." Armstrong admired Glaser's charisma.

After Armstrong switched from the Sunset to a new Chicago hot spot, the Savoy Ballroom, he stopped working with Glaser. Yet the two would meet again.

Chapter 6

"This One's For You, Rex"

The music industry has always been fickle. What might be the hot new music or nightclub one day can lose popularity within months. That was what happened to the Savoy Ballroom. With fewer people coming to the Savoy, the owner had trouble paying Armstrong and his band members. He promised to pay his musicians when things improved, but Armstrong did not know how much longer he could work for free.

Meanwhile Armstrong was still recording for Okeh. One of Okeh's representatives, Tommy Rockwell, was based in New York City. Rockwell urged Armstrong to move back to New York, where jazz was now the biggest thing in live entertainment. Thanks to records and radio, Armstrong was becoming well known outside Chicago. His voice and trumpet were heard by people all over the nation.

Rockwell was so impressed with Armstrong that he wanted the trumpet player to come without his band members. Regardless of what Rockwell wanted, Armstrong would not leave his band behind. So they all got into their cars and formed a jazz caravan heading east.

Armstrong and his entourage arrived in New York in May 1929. Tommy Rockwell was stunned to see that Armstrong had his band members with him. Armstrong later explained, "So I walked into Mr. Rockwell's office and said, 'Well, I've got my band here.' He [Rockwell] said, 'What do you mean, your band?' I said, 'Well, I've got them anyway,' and he said, 'No use sending them back.'"[1]

Rockwell took on the role of manager for Armstrong and his band. As manager, Rockwell not only arranged for Armstrong to make records, but also to perform live gigs. In return, Rockwell received a percentage of the band's pay. Rockwell got the musicians jobs in several clubs, often in the Harlem section of the city. Despite the fact that Harlem is mostly an African-American neighborhood, a lot of white New Yorkers made the trip there to hear the best in live jazz.

> All those years of playing in Chicago and taking a lead role in his band had given Armstrong the confidence he lacked when he was younger.

This sheet music from the 1920s for "W.C. Handy's St. Louis Blues" featured pictures of Armstrong on its cover.

All those years of playing in Chicago and taking a lead role in his band had given Armstrong the confidence he lacked when he was younger. Tommy Rockwell felt his charming and talented client was ready to tackle something new. He wanted Armstrong to perform on Broadway.

Broadway and other streets around it in New York City comprise the live theater capital of the United States. Most Broadway shows, like most movies, are not successes. However, some have become legendary such as *Oklahoma*, *West Side Story*, *My Fair Lady*, and *Cats*.

The show featuring Armstrong was called *Hot Chocolates*. The name was a reference to the fact that the entire cast consisted of African Americans. By today's standards, the title would likely be considered racist, but that was not so in the 1920s.

Hot Chocolates did not tell a story. It consisted of a series of skits and musical numbers reflecting Harlem life. The girls in the show were called "Hot Chocolate Drops." The boys were "Bon Bon Buddies." *Hot Chocolates* premiered on June 20, 1929, and audiences enjoyed it.

Armstrong did not act in *Hot Chocolates*. He was the lead musician. He played a trumpet solo in the show's breakout hit song, "Ain't Misbehavin,'" written by legendary jazz pianist Fats Waller. Armstrong wrote that the song "would bring down the house, believe me! I believe that great song, and the chance I got to play it, did a lot to make me better known all over the country."[2] "Ain't Misbehavin'" became the best selling record up to that time.[3] To this day "Ain't Misbehavin'" is still performed.

Broadway aside, Armstrong continued to make records and do shows in Harlem night clubs. While some performers would not have had the ambition to work so hard, Armstrong constantly drove himself to the point that he had become the hottest thing in New York City.

He became known for his charismatic and energetic style, which included mugging for the audience, rolling his eyes, and wiping his brow with a white handkerchief. Undiscovered musicians copied his style. They all wanted to be like Louis Armstrong.

It seemed like nothing could go wrong for Armstrong's career. Yet, something did, and it was way beyond his control. The Great Depression began.

With many fans unable to afford to go to clubs, talented musicians were suddenly out of work. Some took jobs completely unrelated to music, becoming cab drivers or tailors. *Hot Chocolates* ended its run on Broadway after six months. Armstrong decided to make a drastic change in his career. He decided a few months into the depression to make a new start and move far from both New York City and Chicago. In May 1930, he bought a ticket for Los Angeles and hopped on a train bound for the Pacific Coast.

Despite the woes of the Great Depression, Armstrong's well-recognized name helped him get work in Los Angeles. Since many club gigs were broadcast over radio,

The Great Depression

On October 29, 1929, a huge rush of stockholders sold their stocks in a panic. Suddenly, the values of a large amount of stocks were worthless. Many Americans who had invested their life savings in the stock market were now penniless. Businesses were forced to close in huge numbers. Millions of people had to live on the streets because they could no longer afford homes. Many of those had no money for food.

It was common in cities and towns across the United States to see homeless people living in crude shelters made of tin and cardboard. Others slept outdoors and covered themselves with newspapers.

David Ginsburg was an attorney who worked for President Franklin Roosevelt, who succeeded President Herbert Hoover in 1933. Ginsburg said, "There's only one word that adequately describes it [the Great Depression] and that's surely 'despair.' The sense of helplessness, the sense of hopelessness . . . there was a sense of fright, a sense of horror."[4] Roosevelt started landmark government assistance programs to both put people back to work and to ensure that such an economic catastrophe did not happen again. The Great Depression did not fully end until the United States entered World War II in 1941.

he reached thousands of people who could not hear him play in person. At the same time, he made records at Okeh's West Coast studio.

Armstrong spent just a short time in Los Angeles, but there were two notable occurrences in his life during that period. He appeared in his first movie, a drama titled, *Ex-Flame*. It was released at the end of 1930. Armstrong played himself in a small part, but *Ex-Flame* was not a success. Yet it was the first time tens of thousands of people got to see Armstrong blow his horn.

The other milestone was nothing to be proud of. In November 1930, he was arrested for possession of marijuana. Armstrong was taken to the Los Angeles City Jail where he spent the next nine days.[5] At his trial, Armstrong was given a six-month suspended sentence.[6] News of the sentencing hit the newspapers in Chicago. However, the Chicago papers mistakenly left out the fact that the sentence was suspended.

> Armstrong was taken to the Los Angeles City Jail where he spent the next nine days.

Armstrong left Los Angeles in March 1931 and spent the next few years touring the country performing live. First, he returned to Chicago where his friends were stunned to see good old Satchelmouth. They thought he was in jail in Los Angeles.

It did not take long for Armstrong to get regular gigs at Chicago's Regal Theater. He also moved back with his wife, Lil, for a short time. But their marriage was all but over. The couple separated in August 1931, although they did not officially divorce. That meant neither was legally able to remarry.

Armstrong managed to keep working during the Great Depression by recording music people wanted to buy with the little leisure money they had. He did not experiment much with new styles during these years. What became known as the big-band era was beginning and Armstrong took full advantage of it by playing and recording the fast-paced, swing music. He also played popular sentimental ballads if that's what his audiences wanted.

One of these songs reeks of controversy. To some, the lyrics celebrated the stereotypes white people had of African Americans. It is titled, "When It's Sleepy Time Down South" and was recorded in 1931. The song was a nostalgic look at southern plantation life. It includes lyrics referring to African Americans as "mammies" and "darkies." Those words were used by whites to demean African Americans. Yet Armstrong refused to change them. Not only that, but "When It's Sleepy Time Down South" eventually became Armstrong's theme song.

To Armstrong, the song was simply the tale of a man like himself who left the South to make good in the North. While Armstrong enjoyed his successes in Chicago, New

York, and Los Angeles, he missed the soft breezes and tranquil life of the South of his childhood.

Musicians embark on concert tours for several reasons. One is to appeal to fans who otherwise would not have a chance to hear them play. Another is to give themselves publicity. The more people hear them play, the more records they are likely to buy. Armstrong hired a new manager named Johnny Collins, and under Collins' direction Armstrong went on tour.

In early June 1931, Armstrong arrived for a show in New Orleans. It was his first visit to his hometown in nine years. His mother Mayann had died in 1927, but his sister, Mama Lucy, was there to greet him. He also encountered Joseph Jones and Peter Davis from the waif's home. Jones and Davis asked their former student if he would make a visit to the home, and Armstrong was glad to do so.

Armstrong took a walk through the dormitory where he had once lived. When he found his old bunk he crawled under the sheets and actually fell asleep. He also donated radios to the current residents and took time to pose for pictures with them.

Not all the stops were as pleasant. Legal segregation ruled the South in the 1930s. In Memphis, a bus driver refused to permit Armstrong and his band to board his bus. The Memphis police sided with the bus driver and enforced the segregation laws. The entire band was hauled off to jail. A local theater manager bailed them out.

Louis Armstrong—front, fifth from left—sits with members
of his band at the school he once attended, the
Colored Waif's Home in New Orleans, Louisiana.

Johnny Collins decided that after touring the United States, it was about time Armstrong entertained his European fans. Armstrong, his band, and his female friend Alpha Smith sailed out of New York on July 9, 1932, and arrived by boat in Plymouth, England, on July 14. Even in England, Armstrong encountered discrimination. Several hotels in London would not provide lodging to African Americans.

European audiences loved him, though. Jazz might have been an American-made form of music but it had sure caught on in England. Armstrong did shows for about four months in England and Scotland. One critic called him a wizard with the trumpet. Another said he was the best thing the United States had ever sent to Europe. Not all were kind, and some were truly racist. One British critic, Hannen Swaffer, said of Armstrong, "He looks, and behaves, like an untrained gorilla."[7]

One concert was for a special audience, King George V of England. Playing for British royalty is an honor. Those selected to play for the royals must follow strict rules, called protocol. One is that they must not refer to members of the Royal family while performing. Armstrong broke protocol by announcing before one number, "This one's for you, Rex."[8] ("Rex" is Latin for "king.") Not many people could have gotten away with that, but Armstrong was charming enough to do so without a problem.

One writer named Percy Brooks worked for a British magazine titled *Melody Maker*. He had heard Armstrong referred to by other musicians as Satchelmouth. A British man, Brooks did not fully understand the American Southern accent. He thought people were calling Armstrong Satchmo. So when Brooks met Armstrong in London, he greeted him as "Satchmo." Armstrong liked the new nickname and kept it. From then on, Louis Armstrong was often referred to as Satchmo.

In the 1930s, Armstrong (right) began to play with big bands.

Armstrong sailed back to the United States in November 1932. He arrived in New York harbor on November 9 at 2:30 in the afternoon. True to his nature, he refused to rest. Even though he was exhausted from the long voyage across the Atlantic Ocean, Armstrong did a show that night at a Harlem, New York, nightclub called Connie's Inn. Well-known record producer John Hammond wrote, "Louis Armstrong is back. I have seen him at Connie's the night he arrived, looking better than I have seen him in years."[9]

Armstrong made a few new records in New York but before long was back on the road. He again toured the United States. Then in late July 1933, he sailed to Europe. His friend Alpha Smith and his manager Johnny Collins traveled with him. As before, Armstrong opened his tour in London. In mid-August, Armstrong received word that his father, Willie, had died at the age of forty-nine. Armstrong chose not to attend the funeral of the father who had walked out on his family.

Some of Satchmo's most enthusiastic audiences were in Scandinavia. About ten thousand fans greeted Armstrong at the train station when he arrived in Copenhagen, Denmark. In May 1934, Armstrong and Alpha traveled to Paris. They stayed there for several months, renting an apartment. Much of that time Armstrong did not perform. The years of trumpet playing had taken a toll on his lips. He spent his days in Paris resting his sore lips and socializing with other African-American musicians who settled there, such as trumpet player Arthur Briggs and singer/dancer Josephine Baker.

> The years of trumpet playing had taken a toll on his lips.

By October, Armstrong felt his lips had healed enough to allow him to blow his trumpet once more. He did live shows in some of Paris' hottest clubs. However, near the end of 1934, his lips again became sore. Armstrong was forced to cancel all his pending performances in Europe. In January 1935, he and Alpha boarded a ship and headed back to the United States.

Armstrong settled back in Chicago and rested until May 1935. Tired of dealing with managers he felt were not capable, Armstrong wanted someone tough to watch out for him, just as "Black Benny Williams" had years earlier. There was one person to fit that role. That was Joe Glaser, who Armstrong had met at the Sunset Café in 1927. Armstrong and Glaser would work together until Glaser died in 1969.

Chapter 7

On The Road and Inside Town Hall

rmstrong knew of Glaser's background with organized crime. But Armstrong had grown up with tough guys who had criminal records, so he was not bothered by that part of Glaser's life. It was Armstrong's nature to always look for the good in people.

Glaser got busy right away helping Armstrong's career. First, he signed Armstrong to a new record label, Decca. He arranged for Armstrong to do a four-month stint at Connie's Inn from the late fall of 1935 into the winter of 1936.

Armstrong also released his first autobiography, *Swing That Music*, named for one of his songs. The book was published on November 7, 1936. Many jazz historians today do not put much faith in the book. They say that Armstrong's editors changed his words quite a bit. Still, the book includes information about his background that people had not heard up to that time.

Then in 1937, Glaser sent Armstrong on another American tour. Again, Armstrong ran into discrimination. In some Southern cities, he and his band were not allowed to stay in hotels. Their bus driver would pull over on the side of a road, and the band would spend the night sleeping on the bus. Armstrong played in nightclubs in which he was not allowed to use the bathroom. In other communities, the band was not allowed to enter restaurants.

Joe Glaser made a point to travel with Armstrong and his band in the South since he knew African-American musicians would run into problems there. In those areas where Armstrong's band was not allowed in restaurants, Glaser went out of his way to buy food and bring it to the musicians on the bus. Glaser's special effort was what Armstrong meant about finding the good in people.

Glaser decided to get Armstrong exposure by putting him in movies. Few people saw Armstrong's first movie, *Ex-Flame*, so film was still a relatively untested form of entertainment for Armstrong. Glaser got Armstrong a part in a 1936 movie titled, *Pennies From*

> Glaser got Armstrong a part in a 1936 movie titled, *Pennies From Heaven.*

◆◆◆◆◆◆◆◆◆◆

Bing Crosby

He was born Harry Lillis Crosby in Tacoma, Washington on May 3, 1903, and by the time of his death on October 14, 1977, Bing Crosby was one of the world's best loved entertainers. He is regarded as the greatest of the crooners, singers who interpreted popular standards in an easy and relaxed manner.

Crosby first became nationally known as a solo singer for an early big-band leader, Paul Whiteman. Crosby's smooth stylings made him the standout of Whiteman's band. In 1932, Crosby starred in his first major movie, *The Big Broadcast Of 1932*. By the time he and Armstrong acted together in 1936, Bing Crosby was a household name.

Crosby became as loved for his acting as for his singing. He won an Academy Award in 1944 for best actor in a movie for his role as a priest in *Going My Way*. However, Crosby is likely best remembered for the movies he made as part of a team with another legendary entertainer, Bob Hope. Crosby's 1942 recording of the holiday season classic, "White Christmas," is one of the best selling records of all time.

Heaven. The movie had two established stars: Armstrong and Bing Crosby.

Pennies From Heaven is a heartwarming fantasy about a singer named Larry Poole, played by Crosby, who tries to find a home for a poor grandfather and his granddaughter. Poole inherits a mansion and allows the girl and her grandfather to move in with him. After learning the mansion is haunted, Poole takes advantage of that quirk and turns it into a nightclub called the Haunted House Café.

Armstrong plays a trumpet player named Henry who Poole hires to perform at this oddball café. The role was perfect for Armstrong. He got to clown around on stage and mug for the camera, just as he did for live audiences.

By today's standards, *Pennies From Heaven* seems racist. Armstrong's character fits many old-time stereotypes of African Americans. One common one is that African Americans are superstitious and have an unnatural fear of graveyards. In one scene, Armstrong plays a song titled, "The Skeleton in the Closet." Beside him on screen is a frightening, dancing skeleton. Henry is also portrayed as a simple man who cannot do basic arithmetic.

Some modern jazz historians have questioned why Armstrong played what are today seen as demeaning roles. But in the 1930s, such parts were the only ones African Americans were offered.

The movie was successful and paved the way for more Armstrong film roles. The next year, 1937, he was featured

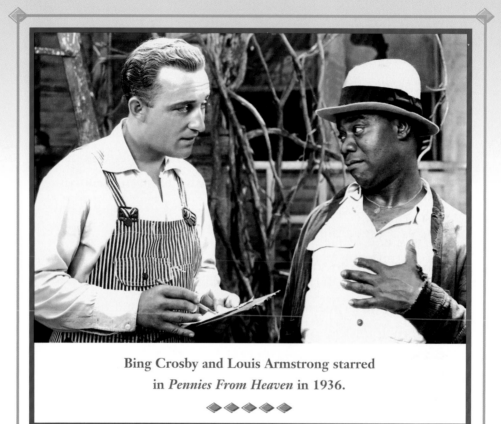

Bing Crosby and Louis Armstrong starred
in *Pennies From Heaven* in 1936.

in a comedy titled *Artists and Models*, starring legendary entertainer Jack Benny. Again, Armstrong played a bandleader.

Glaser also pushed Armstrong into another medium: network radio.

Numerous radio programs included the name of their main sponsor, or biggest advertiser, in their title. A popular musical program of the day was *The Fleischmann's Yeast Hour*, broadcast on the CBS radio network. On April 9, 1937, Armstrong substituted for the program's host, Rudy

The Glory Days of Radio

From the 1920s into the 1950s, people listened to radio the way they watch television today. That period is known as the Golden Age of Radio.

On November 2, 1920, the first commercial radio broadcast aired coverage of the presidential election in which Warren G. Harding beat James Cox. It did not take long for radio to be used for entertainment as well as news. Some of the earliest radio shows were little more than collections of short performances, with comedians alternating with musical acts.

Radios were not small like those today, but were big, bulky console furniture. Some more intricate ones included built-in record players.

By the 1930s and 1940s, radio entertainment had become more sophisticated. Families gathered around radio sets in their living rooms to hear regularly scheduled shows consisting of sketch comedy, musical variety, mystery stories, quiz shows, and romantic soap operas. Radio was also the source for live news. Millions of Americans first heard about the major events of World War II on live radio.

With the growing popularity of television in the early 1950s, the nature of radio began to change. It began to concentrate on live talk and music. The glory days of radio were over.

Vallee. That made him the first African American to host a sponsored national radio program.[1]

That milestone was lost on a certain segment of radio listeners. True, Armstrong was a big star. But most of his fans who were in their teens and twenties when Armstrong first made records were approaching middle age by this time. Young people preferred newer musicians who played swing jazz.

Swing bands were much larger than the bands of five or seven musicians that Armstrong fronted. Most consisted of about fifteen members. The base for swing music was a strong rhythm section that supported solos by horn players. Whether or not a particular swing song was up-tempo or a ballad, the music seemed to be just made for dancing.

Among the best known swing jazz band leaders were Duke Ellington, Count Basie, Artie Shaw, Glenn Miller, and Chick Webb. However, the unofficial king of all swing band leaders was a clarinet player from Chicago named Benny Goodman. It was Goodman who moved jazz into the mainstream when he played a concert in New York City's Carnegie Hall on January 16, 1938. Carnegie Hall had always been a setting for classical music. The idea that jazz had made the move from the honky-tonks of New Orleans to Carnegie Hall was astounding.

To take advantage of the new jazz styles, Armstrong formed his own big band. Yet most jazz historians say he

This poster advertised Louis Armstrong as a star
of radio as well as the live stage and movies.

never really felt comfortable fronting a big band. The music he performed with his big band is not considered his best.

While Armstrong's public image was fading, his private life was on the upswing. Although he and Lil were no longer together as a couple, they were still officially married. That changed when they divorced on September 30, 1938. Less than two weeks later, on October 11, Armstrong married his longtime girlfriend Alpha Smith.

> Shortly after his marriage to Alpha, Armstrong got an extended gig at the renowned Cotton Club in Harlem.

While Lil tended to be serious and focused on her work, Alpha loved to party. Armstrong said that she was too interested in material things, like stylish clothes and fancy jewelry.[2] The two argued much of the time. The marriage was troubled from the start.

Shortly after his marriage to Alpha, Armstrong got an extended gig at the renowned Cotton Club in Harlem. It was not long before one of the regular club dancers caught his eye. She was a twenty-four-year-old African-American woman who went by the stage name of Brown Sugar. Her real name was Lucille Wilson.

Lucille's background was a bit similar to that of Armstrong's second wife, Lil. She was from a stable, middle-class home. Her father owned a cab service based in the New York City borough of Queens. Lucille had taken the job as a Cotton Club dancer to help her family during the Great Depression.

In addition to dancing, she earned money by selling cookies to Cotton Club employees. One time Armstrong bought an entire box from her and distributed them to children living in Harlem.

It was not long before the two were going out to clubs and movies together. Louis loved hopping in the backseat of his classy Packard as his chauffeur drove him and Lucille through the streets of New York. The Packard was a stately car that Armstrong could afford to own now that he was working regularly.

Armstrong was still married to Alpha. She decided to charge Louis five dollars as a kind of penalty fee whenever he came home late from work. She was aware that if he was late he was most likely out hitting the hot spots in town. Armstrong had no problem paying Alpha's fine as long as he could spend time with Lucille.[3]

Meanwhile, Armstrong tried his hand again at Broadway, playing Bottom in an all-African-American musical variation of Shakespeare's *A Midsummer Night's Dream*. It was titled *Swingin' the Dream* and was set in 1890 Louisiana. The show opened on November 29, 1939 to high hopes. However, it was a complete failure, lasting only thirteen performances.[4] Critics blamed the weak script for its failure. It was also a very expensive play to produce.

After the United States entered World War II in December 1941, show business people did their part to support the war by entertaining military personnel. Armstrong was no different. Instead of performing in nightclubs, he did shows at military bases and army hospitals. Armstrong also played at war bond fund raisers. War bonds were a kind of government investment that citizens purchased to help pay for war expenses. Armstrong earned much less for playing these gigs than he did at nightclubs.

While Armstrong was busy performing, his uneasy personal life continued to make news. His marriage to Alpha was crumbling, and the couple divorced on October 2, 1942. On October 12 Armstrong married Lucille Wilson. Armstrong had been married and divorced three times, but his marriage to Lucille was special. They stayed married until Armstrong died.

Armstrong was on the road so much during the 1940s that he did not have a permanent home. He had lived in and out of hotel rooms for many years and had gotten used to that lifestyle. Lucille, on the other hand, wanted a stable home, and Armstrong understood her wish. While he was traveling from city to city in late 1942 and early 1943, Lucille was in New York City looking for a home.

She chose a house in the neighborhood where she had grown up, Corona, Queens. Lucille wanted to live in a quiet neighborhood, away from all the lights and noise of Manhattan show business. The three-story house in Corona was just what she was looking for. Because of its

Armstrong would be married to Lucille the longest of all his wives. This picture was taken in 1952 as the couple was about to leave for a performance in Germany.

unassuming setting, the Armstrong house seemed more fitting for a businessman than a jazz musician. But it was what Lucille desired. The couple moved in during March 1943. Other African-American jazz musicians followed Armstrong and also moved to Corona.

Never mind that Armstrong was not home much. A lot of the time he was in Los Angeles making movies. One of the best known is *Cabin in the Sky*. It was based on a 1940 Broadway play and is today known as the first musical with an all-African-American cast to be marketed to all audiences. (There had been all-African-American movies marketed mainly to African Americans.)

The cast of *Cabin in the Sky* included the most talented African-American entertainers of the swing era. Aside from Armstrong, the movie featured Ethel Waters, Duke Ellington, and Lena Horne. The show tells the story of a man named Little Joe who seems to be in a constant struggle with good and evil. The plot is a basic battle between God and the devil for Little Joe's soul. Armstrong plays a supporting role known as the Trumpeter, a character who works with the devil and is always trying to cause trouble.

By the second half of the 1940s, the jazz world was going through major changes. The big bands that had made swing music the big thing of the 1930s and early 1940s were disappearing. It became too expensive for managers and club owners to pay the salaries and expenses of so many musicians. Small bands of five or six were replacing the big bands. And while big bands emphasized

Louis Armstrong and Duke Ellington have some fun together.

music over vocals, the stars of these smaller bands were their lead vocalists.

That helped Armstrong, since he was a singer as well as a trumpet player. Like Benny Goodman nine years earlier, Armstrong was given the chance to play jazz at Carnegie Hall. It was a completely different experience for Armstrong. He was used to playing for audiences that would get up and dance to his music. Carnegie Hall is an auditorium rather than a dance hall. Audience members sit still in their seats and simply listen to the music.

Armstrong divided his Carnegie Hall show into two parts. The first was a tip of the hat to the new musical fashion, with Armstrong leading a small combo. After intermission, he returned with his big band. The show pulled in very good reviews, with most critics saying they liked the small group better.

Taking that lead, Satchmo formed a six-piece combo he called Louis Armstrong and the All-Stars. The group's personnel changed over the years, but always consisted of superb musicians. These included trombone player Jack Teagarden, a white man from Texas; clarinetist Peanuts Hucko, a native of upstate New York who had played with Glenn Miller and Benny Goodman; Barney Bigard, another clarinetist and a veteran of Duke Ellington's famous band; pianists Earl "Fatha" Hines and Dick Cary; and drummers Sid Catlett and Cozy Cole. The vocalist most of the time was Velma Middleton, a heavy-set woman who loved clowning on stage as much as Armstrong.

Armstrong performs at Carnegie Hall in April 1947.

Louis Armstrong and the All-Stars debuted at New York's Town Hall on May 17, 1947. Armstrong was in his element, once more playing New Orleans-style jazz with a small band. The audience was impressed. They were also amused one day by an unplanned occurrence: Armstrong introduced the song, "Big Butter and Egg Man" but pianist Dick Cary started playing a different number, "A Monday Date." That threw off the rest of the combo. Armstrong stopped the band, went up to the microphone and announced in a loud voice that the next song was "Big Butter and Egg Man." Cary realized his error and he, Armstrong, and the audience had a good laugh. The mix-up reminded the audience that they were seeing a spontaneous jazz performance and not some over-polished routine.

> Cary realized his error and he, Armstrong, and the audience had a good laugh.

The big band days were gone and critics respected Armstrong's performing once more. A columnist for the major jazz magazine *Down Beat* wrote, "Nearly everyone agrees that Louis Armstrong is the outstanding figure in the history of jazz. The greatest trumpeter, the greatest vocalist, the greatest showman, the greatest influence, just the greatest."[5]

That was not true of everyone, however. A new form of jazz was catching fire, and Armstrong would not be a part of it.

Chapter 8

"Hello, Louis!"

Young jazz fans were not listening to Louis Armstrong in the years following World War II. Nor were they listening to big bands. They were into a new type of jazz known as bebop.

The backgrounds and attitudes of the musicians who played bebop in the late 1940s were different from those of Armstrong and the other New Orleans musicians. For one thing, they saw themselves solely as musicians, not entertainers. They would never be caught on stage mugging and clowning for audiences as Armstrong did. While Armstrong was from the South, the majority of bebop musicians rose out of the New York City jazz scene. While Armstrong steered clear of politics, the beboppers, or boppers, were openly angry at white-controlled society.

In addition, their rejection of Armstrong's style of music and entertainment was not only because they wanted to be taken seriously as musicians. They also felt Armstrong represented the old South, the South of

◆◆◆◆◆◆◆◆◆◆

Bebop

Bebop is a style of jazz meant not for dancing but for listening. Unlike New Orleans Dixieland and swing, its emphasis is not on melody. Improvising, or changing chords in the middle of a melody, is common.

To the ears of traditional jazz fans, bebop seems harsh and disharmonious. It is like presenting modern art to a lover of landscapes. Clearly, bebop is not for everyone. But it has always had devoted fans, referred to as boppers. Some of the best bebop stylists were Dizzy Gillespie, Charlie Parker, Thelonious Monk, and Miles Davis.

another time when African Americans lowered themselves to please white people. When Armstrong rolled his eyes and wiped his brow with a handkerchief on stage, the boppers cringed. They detested his movie roles.

One famous singer, Tony Bennett, explained that Armstrong was a product of his times. Bennett said, "He [Armstrong] was a great actor. But because of the bigotry at that time, they [movie producers] kind of just used him, in the Bing Crosby pictures."[1]

A modern day musician named Matt Glaser summed up Armstrong's attitude. Glaser said,

> He did not distinguish between being an artist and being an entertainer. He was a great artist but he was

there to entertain you. . . . [He was on stage] to have fun. He could almost be like a Vaudevillian and do kind of a low humor routine with Velma Middleton. He could joke with the musicians and the audience. . . . And then he could pick up the trumpet and play something that would bring tears to your eyes. He did not distinguish. And this drove a lot of people nuts.[2]

In February 1949 Armstrong fulfilled a personal dream that boppers did not approve of. He appeared as King of Zulu's parade at Mardi Gras in New Orleans.

Armstrong was among the first performers to take advantage of television. Mellow crooner Perry Como hosted an early television variety show. Armstrong appeared on *The Perry Como Show* soon after it premiered in 1948. Another music artist, guitarist Eddie Condon hosted *Eddie Condon's Floor Show*, which ran from 1949 to 1950. Armstrong guest-starred on Condon's program, too. On these variety shows Armstrong did a shortened version of his live show. He played trumpet and hammed it up with his actions.

Offstage Armstrong was not always as happy as he appeared on stage. In 1953, Joe Glaser arranged for Armstrong to go on a six-week tour with swing era legend Benny Goodman. It seemed like a perfect match—two big-name stars with huge followings. Yet the two got along like whipped cream on a cheeseburger. Armstrong liked to take things easy, especially in rehearsals. Goodman

The Krewe of Zulu

Among the highlights of Mardi Gras are parades with humorous and entertaining floats. The parades are organized by private clubs called krewes. The Krewe of Zulu is predominantly African-American and its parade is annually known as one of the most amusing.

Zulu is also one of the most misunderstood parades, especially among African Americans outside New Orleans. Its float riders are African Americans who dress in grass skirts and hand out coconuts as souvenirs; a Zulu coconut is one of the most prized souvenirs for parade viewers. Zulu float riders also dress in blackface, or paint their faces a very dark shade of black, as white minstrel performers did in the 1800s when they imitated African Americans on stage.

To outsiders, the Zulu riders appear to be playing up to every white stereotype of African Americans in the Old South. However, the dress of the Zulu float riders was originally meant to poke fun at a formal, white-dominated, and very regal krewe called Rex. In an early parade, one Zulu rider mocked Rex by wearing a lard can on his head as a crown and holding a banana stalk as a scepter. Today, Zulu is regarded as a satire of racial stereotypes. Zulu members seem to be saying we are acting the way racists depict African Americans; look at how silly it is.

believed in strict discipline, and was constantly trying to get Armstrong to take rehearsal as seriously as he did.

On top of that, audiences seemed to like Armstrong better. Trombone player Trummy Young, one of Armstrong's All-Stars, said Goodman was resentful of Armstrong's success.[3] The tour ended early when Goodman became ill and had to enter a hospital. Years later, Goodman tried to heal old wounds by inviting the Armstrongs to dinner. Armstrong would not let go of the bitterness, and he refused Goodman's offer.

In December 1953, Armstrong played in Japan for the first time and drew huge crowds. Over the next few years he did shows throughout the United States as well as in Italy, Sweden, the Netherlands, and Great Britain. Although it was never intended, Armstrong had become an unofficial American ambassador of good will.

In one concert before Princess Margaret of England, Armstrong broke protocol as he had at the concert for her grandfather King George, twenty years earlier. Before playing a number titled, "Mahogany Hall Stomp," he smiled and announced, "We're really gonna lay this one on for the princess." Instead of being offended, Princess Margaret loved Armstrong's spirit.[4]

Armstrong also enjoyed writing, and he was often seen taking a break from his concert schedule by writing letters to friends or memoirs of his life. To help his fans learn about his early years, Armstrong wrote a second autobiography,

Louis Armstrong appeared on the cover of the
February 21, 1949 issue of *Time* magazine.

published in 1954. It was titled, *Satchmo: My Life in New Orleans.*

Armstrong appeared in eleven more movies in the 1950s. In addition to recording albums, he also made his first single records. Singles were also known as 45s, because they revolved at forty-five revolutions per minute. Unlike albums, 45s feature just one song on each side. Teenagers from the 1950s into the 1970s could not buy enough 45s. With the invention of compact discs, 45s and all other records became obsolete.

Armstrong released two 45s in 1956. In February, Armstrong's record, "A Theme from The Threepenny Opera," also known as "Mack the Knife," first hit the radio airwaves. It was from a 1928 musical written by Kurt Weill and Bertold Brecht. Later that year, he released "Blueberry Hill," originally a hit for Glenn Miller's band in 1940. Armstrong jazzed up both old songs with his signature New Orleans Dixieland style. Both were modest but not big hits and are basically forgotten today.

Though Armstrong was criticized by some African Americans for kowtowing to a white audience, there is no doubt he was proud of his heritage. In May 1956, he and his All Stars made their first trip to Africa. They arrived in the city of Accra, Ghana, where about ten thousand people welcomed the band. In the city of Leopoldville in the Belgian Congo (today the city of Kinshasa, Congo), locals carried him into the stadium on a canvas throne. The people of Africa truly idolized Satchmo.

Armstrong told reporters there, "I feel at home in Africa. I'm African-descended down to the bone, and I dig the friendly ways these people go about things. I got quite a bit of African blood in me from my grandmammy on my mammy's side and from my grandpappy on my pappy's side."[5]

Although he could still thrill audiences, Armstrong was not the trumpet player he had been in his youth. Years of sinking all his energy into blowing his horn had taken a toll on his lips. Much of the time they were tender and sore.

Louis Armstrong and his band perform with people in Africa in 1957.

Both on records and on stage, Armstrong compensated by emphasizing singing over playing, or not blowing his horn as powerfully as he did in the past.

The trumpet player made a lot of noise in 1957 for something that at first seemed totally out of character. Despite the fact that school integration had been overruled by the United States Supreme Court in 1954, most school districts in the South still

> When he saw the televised news from Little Rock, he was outraged.

practiced segregation. When schools in Little Rock, Arkansas, tried to admit a handful of African Americans in the fall of 1957, mobs of white people gathered in protest. Arkansas Governor Orval Faubus promised he would do all he could to keep Little Rock's schools segregated.

People watching television news programs saw films of white adults badgering and heckling African-American children. In one film clip, a grown white man spit in the face of an African-American schoolgirl.

On September 19, 1957, Armstrong was in Grand Forks, North Dakota. When he saw the televised news from Little Rock he was outraged. He lashed out as he spoke to a local reporter. Armstrong growled, "The way they are treating my people in the South, the government can go to hell."[6] He strongly criticized President Dwight Eisenhower, a very popular president, for not taking a stand against Faubus.

Armstrong explained, "My people—the Negroes—are not looking for anything. We just want a square shake. But when I see on television and read about a crowd in Arkansas spitting on a little colored girl, I think I have a right to get sore."[7]

Armstrong also had harsh words about the people of Little Rock. He told a reporter, "They've been ignoring the Constitution, although they taught it in school. But when they go home their parents tell them differently, saying you don't have to abide by it because we've been getting away with it for a hundred years."[8]

Making those statements was a risky, and some said a foolish move. In parts of the South in 1957, African Americans could be lynched for voicing such opinions. Criticism of Armstrong's voicing his opinion came fast and hard. He was blasted as a troublemaker. Some radio stations refused to play his records.

In response, Armstrong cancelled an upcoming international goodwill tour to the Soviet Union. He was hardly in the mood to promote the United States. He asked publicly, "Do you dig me when I say, 'I have a right to blow my top over injustice?'"[9]

Ultimately, Eisenhower sent federal troops to Little Rock to protect African-American students as they entered the school. Afterwards, Armstrong sent a thank you telegram to the president.

In time, the Little Rock controversy faded and Armstrong again toured the world. That did not stop him from taking further stands on racial issues. He stopped playing in New Orleans because a state law banned integrated musical acts from performing. He said, "I don't care if I ever see that city again. They treat me better all over the world than they do in my hometown. Ain't that stupid? Jazz was born there and I remember when it wasn't no crime for cats of any color to get together and blow."[10]

When things were good, he was still energetic and smiley Satchmo. After arriving in the city of Spoleto, Italy, in 1959, a reporter asked him how his Italian was. Armstrong broke into his famous grin and answered, "Oh, very good." He then paused and said clearly, "Pizza."[11] The reporters on hand roared with laughter.

> They treat me better all over the world than they do in my hometown.

In Spoleto in the early hours of June 23, 1959, Armstrong keeled over in pain in his hotel room. Armstrong's doctor, Alexander Schiff, who always traveled with the entertainer, was called to the musician's room. Schiff ordered Armstrong sent to a hospital.

Armstrong was diagnosed with a massive heart attack. Newspapers reported that he was gravely ill. Some even said Armstrong was dying. Yet, while the heart attack was severe, Armstrong recovered. On June 29 he was released from the hospital. Instead of resting as Schiff suggested, he went to a nightclub in Rome. A couple of days later, he flew back to his home in New York. And on July 4, he again performed live.

By the 1960s, Armstrong was viewed by middle-age and elderly people as an elder statesman of jazz. But if he was viewed by teenagers of the swing era as old-fashioned, to teenagers in the 1960s he was a dinosaur. He represented the music of their parents' generation.

In 1964, the Beatles shot into the world of popular music like a rocket. It seemed as if any song they released turned to gold. Other shaggy-haired British rock bands, such as the Rolling Stones, the Dave Clark Five, and Gerry and the Pacemakers, followed suit with hit after hit on the American music charts.

But the Beatles were the kings. Early in 1964, the Beatles held the number one spot on the national music chart for an incredible fourteen consecutive weeks. If anyone was to dethrone the Beatles, it would likely have been another British band. If not a British artist, then perhaps it would be a popular American band such as the Four Seasons or the Beach Boys. Nobody would have thought it would be a 62-year-old jazz musician who had been making records since the 1920s.

Yet that is what happened. On December 4, 1963, Armstrong and his band recorded the theme song to a Broadway play, *Hello, Dolly!* Armstrong had not even heard of the play before then and originally found the song uninteresting. It was just one of several show tunes he was asked to record.

To inject the song with some Dixieland jazz flair, the arrangers added a banjo to it. The single, "Hello, Dolly!," was released early in 1964 and became a phenomenal hit. "Hello, Dolly!" was the song that booted the Beatles from the top of the chart. It reached number one the week of May 9, 1964.[12] Armstrong finally had the hit single that had evaded him in the 1950s. He later performed the song in the movie of the same name.

Armstrong and Barbara Streisand sing the title song of the film version of *Hello Dolly!* in 1969.

Armstrong continued touring and appearing on television shows. Off the stage, he had gotten accustomed to living in his middle-class Queens neighborhood. A big-name star with Armstrong's money could easily have moved to a wealthier area. But Satchmo was happy hanging around with his neighbors of all races, religions, and ethnic backgrounds. At times kids who lived on his street would stop by to watch television with their famous trumpet-playing neighbor.

On other occasions, Armstrong hosted jazz musicians and music critics at his house. One of his frequent guests was bebop pioneer Dizzy Gillespie, who had once slammed Armstrong for demeaning himself to white audiences. They were now friends, and Gillespie admitted being wrong when he judged Armstrong in the 1940s. He recalled the bold stand Armstrong had taken in 1957 by lashing out against the government over the desegregation crisis in Little Rock.

On August 16, 1967, Armstrong recorded a warm and uplifting ballad titled, "What a Wonderful World." It was released as a single, but did not sell well in the United States. However, it did become a big hit in England.

Armstrong suffered from heart and kidney problems in the late 1960s. But he refused to slow down. In March 1971 he played a two-week gig at a New York City hotel, the Waldorf-Astoria. Although his health was failing, Armstrong never lost his love of performing.

Later that spring, Armstrong suffered another heart attack and never recovered. He died in his sleep on July 6, 1971. His body lay in state at the Seventh Regiment Armory in New York City. Roughly twenty-five thousand people came by to pay their respects. Honorary pall-bearers included the top names in show business such as Frank Sinatra, Ella Fitzgerald, Johnny Carson, and Dizzy Gillespie.

Lucille Armstrong outlived Louis, dying on October 5, 1983. She is buried beside her husband in Flushing Cemetery in Flushing, New York.

In 1987, movie director Barry Levinson took an obscure song that few in the United States had heard and put it on the soundtrack of a movie he was making titled, *Good Morning, Vietnam*. The song was "What a Wonderful World," recorded by Armstrong twenty years earlier. The movie was a hit and suddenly millions of Americans discovered Armstrong's wonderful tune about a wonderful world. The record was re-released and became a moderate radio hit in the United States.

However, the legacy of "What a Wonderful World" is that it continues to be used in movie and television soundtracks and recorded by an huge range of performers. Those who have recorded "What a Wonderful World" include: country/pop artist Anne Murray, punk-rock pioneer Joey Ramone, crooner Tony Bennett, veteran rock star Rod Stewart, and non-traditional country pop singer k. d. lang. In April 2006, young rocker Chris Daughtry,

Above, dancers from the Harlem School of
the Arts hold a replica of the stamp.

◆ ◆ ◆ ◆ ◆

one of the final contestants on the smash television
program, *American Idol*, sang "What a Wonderful World"
in competition. Daughtry was born years after Armstrong
died.

"What a Wonderful World" has become a lasting
tribute to Louis Armstrong. Its lyrics sum up his attitude
toward life. Despite his poverty-stricken youth and the
discrimination he faced, Armstrong enjoyed living in what
he saw as a wonderful world.

In August 2001, Armstrong's hometown, which in the 1960s would not allow Armstrong's integrated band to perform in public, changed the name of its airport to the Louis Armstrong New Orleans International Airport.

Today, jazz musicians show a true appreciation for Armstrong as a talent, not just a showman. Wynton Marsalis, one of today's most respected trumpet players, was just ten years old when Armstrong died. Marsalis said, "You're a trumpet player and you hear Louis Armstrong, and you want to play like him, not because he's black but because that's the greatest trumpet you ever heard. That's what you want to play like."[13]

Phoebe Jacobs, a jazz historian and friend of Armstrong, summed it up another way. She said, "I don't believe Louis Armstrong was a real human being. I still believe that God sent him to this earth to be a special messenger—to make people happy."[14]

Chronology

1901— Louis Daniel Armstrong born on August 4 in New Orleans.

1907— Begins school at Fisk School or Boys.

CA.
1909—First works for Karnofsky family.

1912— Arrested for shooting a gun on New Year's Eve and is sent to Colored Waif's Home.

1913— Plays in Colored Waif's Home band.

1914— Released from Colored Waif's Home on June 16.

1915— Starts sitting in with professional jazz musicians King Oliver and Black Benny Williams.

1918— Marries Daisy Parker.

1919— Begins playing with bandleader Fate Marable on riverboats.

1922— Moves to Chicago to play in King Oliver's Creole Jazz Band; divorces Daisy Parker.

1923— Makes first phonograph records with Oliver's band.

1924— Marries Lil Hardin on February 24; arrives in New York City to play in Fletcher Henderson's Band; moves back to Chicago.

1925— Begins recording as Louis Armstrong and His Hot Five (also Hot Four and Hot Seven.)

1929—Moves back to New York City in May.

1929—Broadway play *Hot Chocolates* opens on June 20.

1930—Moves to Los Angeles in May; appears in first movie, *Ex-Flame*.

1931— Moves back to Chicago in March; performs in New Orleans in June, first time in hometown in nine years; separates from but does not divorce Lil Hardin.

1932—Arrives in England on July 14 for first European tour.

1932–1935—Tours extensively in United States and Europe.

1935—Settles back in Chicago; hires Joe Glaser as manager.

1936—Publishes first autobiography, *Swing That Music*, on July 7.

1937— Appears on *The Fleischmann's Yeast Hour* on April 9, the first African American to host a sponsored, nationally broadcast radio program.

1938—Officially divorces Lil Hardin on September 30; marries Alpha Smith on October 11.

1939—*Swingin' The Dream* opens on Broadway on November 29.

1942— Divorces Alpha Smith on October 2; marries Lucille Wilson on October 12.

1943— Buys with Lucille home in Queens section of New York City, which will be his home for rest of life.

1947— Louis Armstrong and the All Stars debut at New York City's Town Hall on May 17.

1949—Appears as king of Zulu in Mardi Gras in New Orleans.

CHRONOLOGY

LATE
1940s—Begins appearing on new popular medium, television.

1953—Opens first tour in Japan in December.

1954—Second autobiography, *Satchmo: My Life in New Orleans* is published.

1956—Releases two singles that become moderate hits; makes first trip to Africa in May.

1957—Angrily speaks out against government handling of integration crisis in Little Rock in September.

1959—Suffers heart attack on June 23 in Spoleto, Italy.

1964—Armstrong single, "Hello Dolly!" dethrones string of Beatles' hits as the number one song in the United States on May 9.

1967—Records "What a Wonderful World" on August 16.

1971—Dies in New York City on July 6.

1987—"What a Wonderful World" is heard in movie, *Good Morning, Vietnam*, becoming radio hit sixteen years after Armstrong's death.

2001—New Orleans' airport gets the new name Louis Armstrong New Orleans International Airport.

Louis Armstrong's Music

A SELECTED LIST

*You can hear the music of Louis Armstrong
on the following compact discs.*

Ambassador Satch (Columbia, 2003)

The Best Live Concert (Verve, 2001)

Louis and the Angels (Verve, 2001)

Satchmo: A Musical Autobiography (Verve, 2001)

Disney Songs, the Satchmo Way (Disney, 2001)

Louis and the Good Book (Universal, 2001)

Satchmo the Great (Columbia/Legacy, 2000)

The Definitive Louis Armstrong (Columbia/Legacy, 2000)

The Katanga Concert (Milan, 2000)

The Glorious Big Band Years, 1937–1941 (EPM, 2000)

The Ultimate Collection (Verve, 2000)

The Complete Hot Five and Hot Seven Recordings
     (Columbia/Legacy, 2000)

Louis Armstrong Sings Back Through the Years
     (MCA Records, 2000)

The Fabulous Louis Armstrong (RCA Victor, 1999)

The Best of Louis Armstrong (MCA Records, 1999)

The Best of Louis Armstrong (Intersound, 1998)

LOUIS ARMSTRONG

Louis Armstrong: An American Icon (Hip-O Records, 1998)

The Complete RCA Victor Recordings (RCA Victor, 1997)

Live at Winter Garden, NY and Blue Note, Chicago (Storyville, 1997)

Now You Has Jazz: Louis Armstrong at M-G-M (Rhino Records, 1997)

Christmas through the Years (Delta, 1996)

What a Wonderful World (GRP Records, 1996)

Radio Days (Moon Records, 1995)

Louis Armstrong's All Time Greatest Hits (MCA Records, 1994)

Swing that Music (Drive Archive, 1994)

Sixteen Most Requested Songs (Columbia/Legacy, 1994)

The Complete Decca Studio recordings of Louis Armstrong and the All Stars (Mosaic Records, 1993)

"What a Wonderful World"—The Elisabethville Concert (Milan, 1993)

The California Concerts (Decca Jazz, 1992)

The Complete Town Hall Concert (RCA Records, 1992)

Louis Armstrong and King Oliver (Milestone Records, 1992)

The Essence of Louis Armstrong (Columbia/Legacy, 1991)

Louis Armstrong and the Blues Singers (Affinity AFS, 1991)

Louis Armstrong: An American Songbook (Verve, 1991

Filmography

A SELECTED LIST

Ex-Flame, 1930

Pennies from Heaven, 1936.

Artists and Models, 1937

Every Day's a Holiday, 1938

Going Places, 1938

Cabin in the Sky, 1943

Jam Session, 1944

Atlantic City, 1944.

New Orleans, 1947

A Song is Born, 1948

Here Comes the Groom, 1951

La botta e riposta, 1951

Glory Alley, 1952

The Glenn Miller Story, 1954

High Society, 1956

The Five Pennies, 1959

La paloma, 1959

Paris Blues, 1961

A Man Called Adam, 1966.

Hello, Dolly!, 1969

Chapter Notes

Chapter 1. The Telegram

1. Ellis L. Marsalis, "New Orleans Jazz Funerals," *American Visions*. October–November 1998, http://www. findarticles.com/p/articles/mi_m1546/is_n5_v13/ai_ 21277702 (May 6, 2006).

2. Louis Armstrong, *Satchmo: My Life in New Orleans* (New York, Signet Books, 1954), p. 179.

Chapter 2. Fish Head Stew, Red Beans, and Rice

1. Louis Armstrong, *Satchmo: My Life in New Orleans* (New York, Signet Books, 1954), p. 13.

2. Ibid.

3. James Lincoln Collier, *Louis Armstrong: An American Genius* (New York: Oxford University Press, 1983), p. 27

4. Joshua Berrett, editor, *The Louis Armstrong Companion: Eight Decades of Commentary* (New York: Schirmer Books, 1999), p. 10.

5. Ibid., p. 5.

Chapter 3. Satchelmouth From Perdido Street

1. Louis Armstrong, *Satchmo: My Life in New Orleans* (New York, Signet Books, 1954), p. 8.

2. Ibid., p. 30

3. Laurence Bergreen, *Louis Armstrong: An Extravagant Life* (New York: Broadway Books, 1997), p. 69.

4. Ibid.

5. Armstrong, *Satchmo: My Life in New Orleans*, p. 33.

6. Louis Armstrong, *Swing That Music* (New York: Da Capo Press, 1936, 1964, 1993) p. 7.

7. Armstrong, *Satchmo: My Life in New Orleans*, p. 41.

8. Ibid.

9. Bergreen, p. 80.

10. Armstrong, *Satchmo: My Life in New Orleans*, pp. 47–48.

11. Michael Meckna, *Satchmo: The Louis Armstrong Encyclopedia* (Westport, Conn.: Greenwood Press, 2004), p. 8.

12. Armstrong, *Swing That Music*, p. 25.

Chapter 4. Fate Steps In

1. Louis Armstrong, *Satchmo: My Life in New Orleans* (New York, Signet Books, 1954), p. 120.

2. Ibid.

3. Laurence Bergreen, *Louis Armstrong: An Extravagant Life* (New York: Broadway Books, 1997), p. 148.

4. Ibid., p. 149.

5. Thomas Brothers, editor, *Louis Armstrong: In His Own Words* (New York: Oxford University Press, 1999), p. 83.

6. Bergreen, p. 169.

7. Ibid.

8. Louis Armstrong, *Swing That Music* (New York: Da Capo Press, 1936, 1964, 1993) p. 69.

Chapter 5. Up North

1. Louis Armstrong, *Swing That Music* (New York: Da Capo Press, 1936, 1964, 1993) p. 70.

2. Ibid.

3. James Lincoln Collier, *Louis Armstrong: An American Genius* (New York: Oxford University Press, 1983), p. 94.

4. Armstrong, *Swing That Music*, p. 71.

5. Joshua Berrett, editor, *The Louis Armstrong Companion: Eight Decades of Commentary* (New York: Schirmer Books, 1999), p. 38.

6. Michael Meckna, *Satchmo: The Louis Armstrong Encyclopedia* (Westport, Conn.: Greenwood Press, 2004), p. 58.

7. Berrett, *The Louis Armstrong Companion: Eight Decades of Commentary*, p. 38.

8. Collier, p. 113.

9. Joshua Berrett, *Louis Armstrong & Paul Whiteman: Two Kings of Jazz*, (New Haven, Conn.: Yale University Press, 2004), p. 54.

10. Laurence Bergreen, *Louis Armstrong: An Extravagant Life* (New York: Broadway Books, 1997), p. 260.

11. Ibid.

12. Berrett, *Louis Armstrong & Paul Whiteman: Two Kings of Jazz*, p. 42.

13. Meckna, p. 321.

14. Gary Giddins, writer; Toby Bryan, producer, *Satchmo: Louis Armstrong*, videotape, (CMV Enterprises, 1986)

Chapter 6. "This One's For You, Rex"

1. Louis Armstrong, *Swing That Music* (New York: Da Capo Press, 1936, 1964, 1993) p. 89.

2. Ibid, p. 91.

3. "Louis Armstrong: The Man, the Musician, the Celebrity," *Kennedy Center*, <http://artsedge.kennedy-center.org/exploring/louis/scrapbook/bio_detail.html> (February 3, 2006).

4. *The American Experience: FDR*, videotape (David Grubin Productions, 1994)

5. Joshua Berrett, editor, *The Louis Armstrong Companion: Eight Decades of Commentary* (New York: Schirmer Books, 1999), p. 81.

6. Ibid.

7. Laurence Bergreen, *Louis Armstrong: An Extravagant Life* (New York: Broadway Books, 1997), p. 355.

8. Albin Krebs, "Louis Armstrong" chapter from *New York Times: Great Lives of the Twentieth Century*, edited by Arthur Gelb, A.M. Rosenthal, and Marvin Siegel, (New York: Times Books, 1988), p. 7.

9. James Lincoln Collier, *Louis Armstrong: An American Genius* (New York: Oxford University Press, 1983), p. 255.

Chapter 7. On The Road and Inside Town Hall

1. Michael Meckna, *Satchmo: The Louis Armstrong Encyclopedia* (Westport, Conn.: Greenwood Press, 2004), p. 105.

2. Ibid., p. 10.

3. Laurence Bergreen, *Louis Armstrong: An Extravagant Life* (New York: Broadway Books, 1997), p. 394.

4. Meckna, p. 294.

5. Bergreen, p. 435.

Chapter 8. "Hello, Louis!"

1. Gary Giddins, writer; Toby Bryan, producer, *Satchmo: Louis Armstrong*, videotape, (CMV Enterprises, 1986)

2. *Jazz*, a film by Ken Burns, written by Geoffrey V. Ward, episode 9: "The Adventure," Florentine Films, 2000

3. Joshua Berrett, editor, *The Louis Armstrong Companion: Eight Decades of Commentary* (New York: Schirmer Books, 1999), p. 125.

4. Albin Krebs, "Louis Armstrong" chapter from *New York Times: Great Lives of the Twentieth Century*, edited by Arthur Gelb, A.M. Rosenthal, and Marvin Siegel, (New York: Times Books, 1988), p. 7.

5. Ibid.

6. Laurence Bergreen, *Louis Armstrong: An Extravagant Life* (New York: Broadway Books, 1997), p. 471.

7. Ibid., p. 472.

8. *Jazz*, episode 9: "The Adventure."

9. "Louis Armstrong: A Cultural Legacy," *Smithsonian Institution*, <http://www.npg.si.edu/exh/armstrong> (December 31, 2005).

10. "Louis Armstrong: The Man, the Musician, the Celebrity," *Kennedy Center*, <http://artsedge.kennedy-center.org/exploring/louis/scrapbook/bio_detail.html> (February 3, 2006).

11. Giddins

12. Fred Bronson, *The Billboard Book Number 1 Hits*, (New York: Billboard Books, 2003), p. 146.

13. *Jazz*, episode 2: "The Gift."

14. Ibid.

Further Reading

———◦/◦/◦———

BOOKS ON LOUIS ARMSTRONG

Cogswell, Michael. *The Offstage Story of Satchmo.* Portland, Ore.: Collectors Press, Inc., 2003.

Collier, James Lincoln. *The Louis Armstrong You Never Knew.* New York: Children's Press, 2004.

Holland, Gini. *Louis Armstrong.* Milwaukee, Wis.: World Almanac Library, 2004.

McDonough, Yona Zeldis. *Who Was Louis Armstrong?* New York: Grosset & Dunlap, 2004.

Raum, Elizabeth. *Louis Armstrong: Jazz Legend.* Mankato, Minn.: Capstone Press, 2006.

BOOKS ON JAZZ

Asirvatham, Sandy. *The History of Jazz.* Philadelphia: Chelsea House Publishers, 2003.

Kallen, Stuart A. *The History of Jazz.* San Diego: Lucent Books, 2003.

Martin, Marvin. *Extraordinary People in Jazz.* New York: Children's Press, 2004.

McCurdy, Ronald. *Meet the Great Jazz Legends.* Van Nuys, Ca.: Alfred Publishing Co., 2004.

Ward, Geoffrey and Burns, Ken. *Jazz: A History of America's Music.* New York: Alfred A. Knopf, 2005.

BOOKS ON MUSIC AND THE ARTS

Hill, Laban Carrick. *Harlem Stomp!: A Cultural History of the Harlem Renaissance.* New York: Little, Brown, 2003.

Orgill, Roxana. *Shout, Sister, Shout! Ten Girl Singers Who Shaped a Century.* New York: Margaret K. McElderry Books, 2001.

Tate, Eleanora E. *African American Musicians.* Ed. Jim Haskins. New York: Wiley, 2000.

Internet Addresses

Satchmo.net

The official site of the Louis Armstrong House and Archives.

<http://www.satchmo.net>

PBS Biographies

The official Public Broadcasting System site based on Ken Burns' documentary, Jazz. *This Armstrong-related site has photographs, information, and links to song clips.*

<http://www.pbs.org/jazz/biography/artist_id_
armstrong_louis.htm>

Red Hot Jazz

This site has extensive information on early jazz.

<http://www.redhotjazz.com/>

Index

Page numbers for photographs are in **boldface** type.

INDEX